Foreword by C. Everett Koop, M.D.

Understanding Your Child's Temperament

William B. Carey, M.D.
 The Children's Hospital of Philadelphia
with Martha M. Jablow

MACMILLAN
A Simon & Schuster Macmillan Company
1633 Broadway
New York, NY 10019-6785

Library of Congress Cataloging-in-Publication Data

Carey, William B.
          Understanding your child's temperament / William B. Carey with
    Martha M. Jablow and The Children's Hospital of Philadelphia.
          p.   cm.
          Includes bibliographical references and index.
          ISBN: 0-02-862826-8
          1. Temperament in children. 2. Child rearing. 3. Parenting.
    I. Jablow, Martha Moraghan.   II. Children's Hospital of
    Philadelphia.   III. Title.
    BF723.T53C37   1997
    649'.1—dc21   97-14347
                                                         CIP

Printed in the United States of America
10 9 8 7 6 5 4 3

ACKNOWLEDGMENTS

Several people deserve special recognition for their vital roles in the production of this book. Any errors of fact or opinion are, of course, my fault and not the fault of anyone else.

Shirley Bonnem, Vice President of The Children's Hospital of Philadelphia, welcomed and encouraged this book as an addition to the ongoing series of publications issued by The Children's Hospital to foster parent education. She arranged the congenial working relationship between writer Martha M. Jablow and me. Literary agent Nancy Love is thanked for bringing us to Macmillan. Editor Mary Ann Lynch's help and enthusiasm for this book has been most appreciated.

Catherine J. Andersen of Vancouver, British Columbia, provided me with the initial stimulus to write this book. As the mother of three and the founder of a unique parent support group, she advised me that such a book was needed and urged me to undertake the challenge of making research work and clinical experience available to parents. Kate also reviewed the initial outline and the entire manuscript and made innumerable thoughtful suggestions on how to improve it.

Another essential reviewer was my research and writing partner and friend, Sean C. McDevitt, Ph.D., of Scottsdale, Arizona. Some valuable criticisms came from my wife, Ann McDougal Carey, mother of three children with varied temperaments, and from our daughter, Elizabeth. They provided me with reassurance that I was more or less on the right track and helped me back on when I wandered off.

Stella Chess and Alexander Thomas provided the brilliantly insightful view of temperament that forms the basis of this book. I am enormously indebted to them for this inspiration and for their strong support and friendship throughout the last thirty years. Their wisdom is found in many places throughout the book.

It is no exaggeration to say that, apart from the research literature, my greatest source of information about temperament was the families I had the privilege to know and serve during more than thirty years of general pediatrics practice. I am greatly indebted to these parents and children for all they have taught me.

William B.Carey, M.D.

May 1997

CONTENTS

FOREWORD

By C. Everett Koop, M.D.

I met Dr. William B. Carey more than forty years ago when he began his residency at The Children's Hospital of Philadelphia, where I spent more than thirty-five years as Surgeon-in-Chief. His two-year residency was followed by time in the United States Army. Bill then returned to Children's Hospital because the behavior of children always fascinated him. He took an additional year of training in what was then called psychological pediatrics. Today he is Director of Behavioral Pediatrics in the Division of General Pediatrics at Children's Hospital.

In the intervening years, Dr. Carey was a practicing pediatrician in a nearby suburb of Philadelphia. He often referred his surgical patients and other children who needed special care to us at Children's Hospital. In 1968, he began researching temperament to determine how it affects a child's behavior, development, school performance, physical health, and responses to stress and crisis. He is quick to credit his postresidency period at Children's Hospital as the inspiration for his three decades of work in this area.

The fruit of his extensive research and clinical practice is now available to parents for the first time in *Understanding Your Child's Temperament*. Although Dr. Carey has written widely for physicians and other professionals, this book puts the same valuable information in the hands of parents, and does so in a practical, direct way.

Parents have always found child rearing to be a challenging task. Today parenthood is no less complicated than ever before. In fact, it may even be more so. The complex social forces of our times can be overwhelming for many families. Unfortunately there is no general agreement among experts as to the best techniques for raising children.

A generation or two ago, most pediatric authorities commonly traced any problem in a child's behavior to parents' inadequacies. Some experts still do. For many, though, the pendulum has swung toward the opposite extreme. Parents today are too often told that some sort of abnormality in their child's brain is the cause of problems in social behavior and school performance.

Understanding Your Child's Temperament offers a refreshingly balanced perspective on children, their development, and behavior. Based on Dr. Carey's own research and that of his colleagues, this book presents a view of children's everyday behaviors that should revolutionize parenting for many readers. Dr. Carey adds a great deal of practical pediatric experience to the research findings as well as a good bit of common sense.

He explains what temperament is, why it is significant, and how it affects both children and parents. He shows parents how to recognize and handle a range of different—yet normal—temperament styles. Perhaps more important, he offers solid suggestions for working effectively and harmoniously with a child's inborn temperament. And he helps perplexed parents clarify the distinction between a child's normal temperament variations and behavioral adjustment issues. The ultimate results can diminish family conflicts and prevent or reduce potential behavior problems.

Dr. Carey is highly qualified to discuss temperament. He and a group of psychologists developed a set of five questionnaires that measure variations in temperament. These surveys are available in more than two dozen languages. In the early 1990s, Dr. Carey was recognized by his peers at the American Academy of Pediatrics when he received the C. Anderson Aldrich Award for Child Development and the Practitioner Research Award. He has been the co-editor of two editions of the textbook, *Developmental-Behavioral Pediatrics*. He was elected to the Institute of Medicine of the National Academy of Sciences in 1984.

A few years ago, The Children's Hospital of Philadelphia began to expand its parent education efforts by encouraging the publication of books based on the work of its physicians, nurses, and mental health professionals. Now Dr. Carey contributes to that effort by sharing his insight and knowledge with parents through *Understanding Your Child's Temperament.*

The chief value of this book is that it brings to parents for the first time a comprehensive review of what is known about temperament from infancy through adolescence. Although a few other books on the subject have been published in the last several years, none provides the broad coverage and practical orientation of this book.

Understanding Your Child's Temperament is especially supportive of families. It doesn't blame or label parents or children. Instead, it offers information and guidance based on extensive research, clinical data, and pediatric experience. It is an important book because it brings balance and enlightenment to parents who are trying to raise healthy, well-adjusted, unique children.

PREFACE

A couple recently came to my office at The Children's Hospital of Philadelphia for a consultation. On that mild spring afternoon, Maria and Eric held their six-month-old son, James, who looked quite healthy and content.

So what was the problem that brought them to me? The parents said that their little boy had been "basically screaming since birth." James was their third child, and he was completely unlike their first two children. The parents were visibly tense as they told me that they had not had a good night's sleep since mother and baby had come home from the hospital.

These intelligent, well-educated, mature adults were completely perplexed by this baby. They had searched for explanations for his screaming and found none. Maria's pregnancy and delivery had been free from complications and James was growing and developing well. No physical problems had been found during the several well-baby checkups since his birth.

At first their pediatrician had told them that the problem was colic and had changed the baby to a milk-free formula. But this did nothing for his crying. Numerous long bouts of irritability and crying continued well beyond three months of age, and James was still waking at least three times every night. The parents returned to the pediatrician, reported that changing to milk-free formula had not solved the problem, and asked urgently what else could be done. The pediatrician then arranged for a consultation to rule out a neurological cause for the baby's crying. Fortunately, James's nervous system was found to be completely sound. At that point, the pediatrician's advice was to bear with the problem because the baby would outgrow it.

Eric and Maria, however, were still confused and upset. Other sources of assistance were not particularly helpful. Their family and friends had no experience with a baby such as this one, and some even implied that the mother and father should consider counseling for themselves. They turned to many books on child care but found little useful advice about the sources or solutions for problems such as theirs. They again contacted the neurologist who had found nothing wrong with James's nervous system. She referred them to me for a consultation.

And so they came to see me out of utter frustration. Between the time they had telephoned to schedule an appointment and the consultation itself, I had sent them a questionnaire that asked them for extensive observations of the baby's reactions to their care. From those observations and my discussion with Maria and Eric, it became clear that James was definitely hard to manage, and would be for any parents. They described him as sensitive, irritable, hard to soothe, unpredictable, and intolerant of change.

I helped them understand that these traits are part of their son's temperament; they were not caused by any physical illness and were not anybody's fault. We discussed temperament in general and what it meant in their child's case. Although these parents recognized that their two older children were quite different from each other, they had not realized that their new baby's behavior was just another normal variation. Maria and Eric also recalled how different each of them had always been from their own siblings. As we talked about temperament, it became apparent that these parents, like most parents, had an intuitive understanding of what it is.

When the concept of temperament is first raised, adults grasp it fairly well. In fact, most of us have acquired some insight into our own temperaments. You probably know, for example, how you tend to react when you walk into a room full of strangers. Perhaps you approach people with your hand extended, introduce yourself, and strike up a conversation easily. Or maybe you hang back, shifting your weight from foot to foot, until someone speaks to you first. Your response in this situation tells you something about just one aspect of your temperament. You may be outgoing, or you may tend to be shy and withdrawn. When you face a demanding task at work, do you plunge in and plug away until you complete it? Or are you more likely to procrastinate, taking a lot of breaks, and dragging it out? Your answer indicates something about another aspect of your temperament—your degree of persistence.

The previous examples are only two of nine possible ways of looking at temperament that will be discussed in detail in this book. When asked, many adults will say that they understand their own temperament. Few, however, take their child's temperament into consideration when dealing with him or her.

I reassured the worried parents in my office that day that their child's challenging style of reacting was normal. There was nothing "wrong" with a baby who fussed before falling asleep, or who was highly sensitive. Along with revising their view of this baby's problem, I suggested some different strategies for handling the various distressing behaviors. One of the most important changes was for them to make a shift from feeling angry, guilty, or frightened about James's fussing to trying to figure out when it was a true expression of need and when it was simply fussing. Learning not to overreact to each whimper was an essential part of the new plan for handling their baby. They seemed relieved and eager to try a new approach.

This couple was not at all unusual. I have met hundreds of parents like them during the thirty-one years I have spent in general pediatrics practice. It distresses me to find so many devoted, loving parents trying to do their best for their child but often without sufficient information about normal individual behavioral differences and how to manage them. Whether they are single parents raising a child alone or partners trying to share parental responsibilities, all parents can benefit by a clearer understand of temperament. Yet despite a multitude of books, magazines, videos, and tapes on parenting, little is available on issues such as those confronting the couple in my office that spring afternoon.

A limited amount of information about temperament is available in several books, but either much of the information was obtained before the latest research was available or the book discusses only a particular aspect of this complicated subject. The role and influence of temperament first became available to parents in 1965 with the book *Your Child Is a Person* by Stella Chess, Alexander Thomas, and Herbert Birch. This volume was valuable for introducing information about children's individuality but was published before much of the modern research (including their own) had been completed. In 1969, T. Berry Brazelton also acquainted readers with individual differences in *Infants and Mothers,* a very useful early book but limited in scope for the same reason.

More recently, some helpful books have presented and discussed the more negative aspects of temperament, notably *The Difficult Child* by Stanley Turecki with Leslie Tonner in 1985 (and revised in 1989) and *Raising Your Spirited Child* by Mary Sheedy Kurcinka in 1991. Drs. Chess and Thomas published another instructive book, *Know Your Child,* in 1987 (republished in 1996), which is only partly devoted to temperament.

At the same time, bookstores and libraries have been flooded with books about attention deficit/hyperactivity disorder (ADHD). *Understanding Your Child's Temperament* makes the point that many of the problems now being given this fashionable diagnosis probably have been mislabeled. Many children diagnosed with ADHD do not have that abnormality of the nervous system; rather, their behaviors represent normal variations of temperament that do not fit well with the expectations of schoolteachers, counselors, and administrators.

My reason for writing this book is to offer parents a comprehensive guide that summarizes in a useful form the latest research in the field of children's temperament. In 1995, psychologist Sean McDevitt and I wrote a similar volume for a professional audience of physicians, psychologists, and educators. This book makes the same information accessible to parents and offers suggestions for managing different temperament characteristics.

Unlike other books to date, *Understanding Your Child's Temperament* considers children of all ages, from the newborn to the adolescent. It describes the role of temperament not only with regard to behavioral problems but to physical health, development, school performance, and crisis situations. It deals with the challenging aspects of these traits at both extremes, such as high activity and low activity. And it offers parents a way to identify and understand the nine temperament traits in each child.

Understanding Your Child's Temperament describes my own research findings and many years of clinical experience. Its foundation rests mainly on the work of many other researchers too numerous to list here. A sampling of them includes—in addition to Stella Chess and Alexander Thomas—Judith Dunn, Barbara Keogh, Adam Matheny, Michel Maziade, Roy Martin, Sean McDevitt, and Robert Plomin. My apologies to the many others for whom there is not enough space to mention.

One may ask how I, as a practicing pediatrician, became interested in the subject of temperament. My formal medical training took place in the 1950s when the prevailing psychological theories agreed that differences and problems in children's behavior were all the result of what parents had done or had not done to children—or even what parents had just felt about them. In the real world of practice I discovered that although this was true part of the time, it just did not make any sense with many of the problems I encountered.

In many cases, there was simply no way that a child's behavior could be attributed solely to the parents. There had to be some other factor. When I became acquainted with the work of Drs. Chess and Thomas in 1960, I found the answer. Although temperament does not explain everything, it does make sense of many of the variations previously left unexplained. I have spent many years exploring this important aspect of children and am now finally offering specifically to parents the benefits of that experience and the contributions of many others.

In writing this book, my goal has been to present to parents a large body of information, much of which was previously available only to professionals. My mission is to help you understand what temperament is, how it affects your child and you, how to identify and assess it in your own child, and how to work with it instead of against it. In this way, your child can achieve greater harmony within the family and at school, with other children and adults, and with himself.

The result was happy for the family who came to my office that spring afternoon. In two follow-up discussions on the telephone, Eric and Maria told me that their son was much improved. Because they now had a far greater understanding of the situation, his needs, and his temperament, they felt more relaxed and confident about handling him. James was still a little fussier than their other two children had been, but much less so than he was at the time of the office visit. He was sleeping through the night at last, and so were they.

INTRODUCTION

What Is Temperament?
Why Does It Matter?

AS DIFFERENT AS SNOWFLAKES

Spend ten minutes observing children in a playground, classroom, or your own kitchen. Watch how differently each child interacts with people and responds to objects and events.

Just as every child has individual physical features—voice, smile, hair, the arch of an eyebrow—each has a different temperament, or *style of behavior,* in responding to people, objects, events, and other stimuli. Let's observe three children.

> *As other children dash from dress-up corner to puzzles to blocks, Michael watches quietly from the edge of the room. When he began attending the day care center, he would cling tightly to his mother's or father's hand as they walked inside. Michael would beg them not to leave him. Once his parents departed, he would sob quietly for half an hour. Michael did this every morning for several days but gradually accepted day care as a fact of his life.*
>
> *After a month at the center, Michael now leaves his parents without tears or clinging. He enters the room, hangs up his jacket, and goes off to find something to entertain himself. Michael does not look unhappy; however, he initially resists suggestions from the staff to join other children in group activities. When another child asks him to play a ring-toss game, for example, he declines at first and goes off on his own*

to play with a toy truck. After several minutes, he approaches the other child, picks up a plastic ring, and joins the game.

Michael's teacher recently told his parents that he is "emotionally insecure."

Suzannah comes home from kindergarten and reports that she "hates" her teacher because the teacher "makes us line up and not say a word" before going outside to recess. "She's mean and she has all these dumb rules," Suzannah complains. Her parents are not surprised. Suzannah is bright and funny but often explosive—a little Sarah Bernhardt, as her father calls her—when things do not go her way.

When Suzannah was a toddler, she poured a scoop of sand on another child's head after he demolished her sand castle. She tossed a tantrum in a supermarket when her request for a certain chocolate cereal was denied. Last week, she shoved a larger child when he did not let her cut in line ahead of him.

Some neighbors and parents of Suzannah's playmates have told her parents that Suzannah seems "immature."

"Earth to Andy!" his father calls. Andy is in outer space again, looking out the window at the darkening sky. "Stop daydreaming and get back to your homework."

Andy is in the fourth grade. By now his parents and teachers know that he has an above-average IQ; however, his schoolwork does not reflect his abilities. He forgets to write down his assignments, loses his completed homework, and leaves his schoolbag on the school bus—not once in a while, but frequently. His teachers remark that he does not pay attention in class. Yet he scores well on tests.

At home, Andy seems to be late for everything. He seems never to have finished getting dressed, brushing his teeth, or putting away his toys. His mother must repeatedly tell him to "speed it up" at mealtime, when the bus is due, or whenever the rest of the family is waiting for him in the car.

Over the past four years, Andy's teachers have given him various labels. They say Andy is "hyperactive," "lazy," and "deliberately oppositional."

These three children happen to be brothers and sister. They live in the same home, with the same parents, in the same community. Yet each child has a unique temperament. Although they are different ages, their behavioral style—their temperament—is not determined by their age or stage of development. Nor is temperament determined by their intelligence or other abilities, or by their general emotional and behavioral adjustment.

Temperament should not be confused with personality. It is but one part of personality, which encompasses more dimensions, such as talent, intelligence, emotion, and sense of humor, as well as temperament. Temperament is the stylistic part of personality; it is the distinguishing flavor, style, or characteristic that makes one's personality unique. Temperament refers to the distinct, yet normal, behavioral patterns that we bring to various situations. It affects how we experience and respond to a multitude of environments.

Michael, for example, brings a shy temperament to unfamiliar situations such as a new day care setting. Suzannah brings a spirited, and some would say stubborn, temperament to situations in which she does not get her way and must make adjustments. Andy brings an inattentive, scatterbrained temperament to schoolwork and household tasks whether or not they interest him. He is not hyperactive, lazy, or oppositional. These examples are a bit oversimplified for now; however, we will revisit these children later in this book. We will discover that these characteristics do not make up each child's whole personality but do reveal how Michael, Suzannah, and Andy experience and interact in various challenging situations.

VARIABLE STANDARD EQUIPMENT

Recent research has shown that temperament is largely inborn. For that reason, we need to take a fresh look at how parents and other adults can work *with* a child's temperament, rather than against it. Every baby comes equipped with a unique temperament. From infancy through adulthood, each individual brings his or her own behavioral style to interact with the surrounding environment. For each child, that temperament is *normal,* although interactions with it may have led to problems in function or behavior.

About half of a child's temperament is inherited. The other half comes from a variety of physical and psychological factors in the child and in the environment. These factors include conditions during the mother's pregnancy, such as her nutrition, drug use, or general health; the child's physical health after birth, such as nutrition, medical complications as a newborn, abnormalities of the central nervous system, and exposure to toxins; and psychological influences of the family and other environments.

The fact that temperament is inborn may not be blockbuster news; however, temperament—and its influence on both child and parent—has been widely misunderstood. Many parents think that temperament can be molded or "corrected" with discipline, structure, rewards, and, in too many cases, medication. In effect, they are trying to rewire the child's circuitry. If parents do not understand the inborn nature of temperament, or if they read their child's temperament incorrectly, they unintentionally work against the child's natural behavioral style in trying to change basically unchangeable aspects of behavior. Doing so usually backfires.

Certainly, discipline and structure both have an important place in a parent's arsenal of skills. All children need them, along with demonstrated affection and occasional rewards. These parenting tools are most effective when they are used in concert with the normal predisposition and behavioral styles of children, that is, with their temperaments.

Temperament traits are never completely fixed, and they are never completely changeable either. Although parents cannot change their child's basic temperament, they can alter the way they respond to and manage it. (Ways to do this are discussed in later chapters.)

A NEW UNDERSTANDING:
THE IMPORTANCE OF A "GOOD FIT"

For much of the twentieth century, educators, psychologists, and medical professionals primarily looked to environment for the causes of behavioral differences and problems. Of course, many factors in a child's environment can affect social behavior, school performance, and self-esteem. A child who is loved, well nourished, and healthy, who is given responsibilities and consequences, and who is appropriately stimulated in intellectual, physical, social, and artistic ways, is likely to be happier and have fewer problems than is a child who is abused, unchallenged, or uncared for emotionally and physically.

Yet the exaggeration of environmental influences has led to the neglect of the important role played by inborn temperament. As a result, behavioral problems often have been attributed entirely to the child's environment, that is, to something the parents did or did not do. They were too strict or too lenient. Too attentive or too inattentive. Such overemphasis on external, environmental causes has led to unnecessary parental blame and guilt.

Although we know more about temperament today, research evidence about inborn temperament differences has been misinterpreted in several ways. Some professionals deny that these differences really exist or assign them to "maternal perception" (the mother's imagination). Some say that these differences are present but are trivial or unimportant. Others treat normal temperament as abnormal behavior caused by the parents' mishandling or by brain malfunction.

Sometimes parents bring their concerns about temperament traits to their healthcare professionals only to be told, "It's nothing" or "He will grow out of it." In too many instances, physicians and parents do not differentiate between a child's normal temperament traits, such as inattentiveness or distractibility, and true brain dysfunction. The unfortunate and unnecessary result is misdiagnosis and inappropriate treatment. More about this in Chapter Seven. In most cases of attention deficit/hyperactivity disorder (ADHD) as now diagnosed, there is no documented abnormality of brain function.

A better way of understanding your child's behavioral problems may be to view her temperament as being at odds with her environment. Such an approach would call for accepting her temperament while modifying her surroundings to improve the "fit" between temperament and environment. Ultimately, this fit matters more than the temperament itself. The important concept of "goodness of fit" was the principle finding of the New York Longitudinal Study thirty years ago by psychiatrists Stella Chess and Alexander Thomas.

The goal of this book is to help parents help their child achieve the best possible fit between his or her normal, inborn temperament and the home, school, and social environments. To illustrate this, let's return to Michael for a moment. When the teacher told Michael's parents that he was "emotionally insecure," fortunately they knew enough about temperament in general and Michael's temperament in particular to stay calm. They did not rush him to a therapist because they recognized that his behavioral style—his temperament—was to be shy in new situations. Michael had not been emotionally damaged by his parents. He simply needed to be understood better by his teachers and to have greater respect shown for his individuality.

During a teacher's conference, Michael's parents told the teacher that their son had always been slow to warm up when he was in unfamiliar territory. They suggested that with gentle nudging Michael could be persuaded to take part gradually in group activities. If he did show reluctance, they suggested he be allowed to sit on the sidelines and watch until he felt ready to join. Pushing and prodding him, they warned her, has always been counterproductive because he becomes even more withdrawn. Once Michael felt comfortable, however, he would participate.

Over the following weeks, Michael's teacher invited him to play ball or build blocks with another child or in a small group, but she did not insist. "When you're ready, Michael," she often said. Within a few months Michael had made two new friends and was playing more readily in larger groups of children.

Michael, Suzannah, and Andy's parents understood and accepted individual temperament traits. They did not panic when others labeled Suzannah "immature" or Andy "lazy, oppositional, or hyperactive." They knew that each child has his or her own style of reacting to given situations. These parents had learned to tolerate this individuality and guided their children toward a more harmonious fit between their temperaments and various environments.

HOW TEMPERAMENT MATTERS

It is important to understand temperament for several reasons:

- Temperament profoundly affects the relationship between parent and child.

- Temperament may affect a child's physical health, development, and behavior.

- Temperament influences adults' functioning, both as parents and as individuals.

A child's temperament can have a strong impact on how parents view themselves. Studies have shown, for example, that parents experience distress, helplessness, and diminished self-esteem when their child's temperament is challenging or difficult to tolerate. One study found that women were less likely to return to work in the child's early years if the child had an irritable temperament. Another study looked at marital satisfaction both before the birth of a child and four months after the birth; the conclusions were that certain characteristics of an infant's temperament, such as irregularity and irritability, were associated with a decline in marital satisfaction for both fathers and mothers. Similarly, another investigation found negative personality changes in couples—particularly with regard to their sense of personal control—after the birth of babies who had hard-to-manage temperaments.

Some parents may feel inadequate or guilty when their second child does not go to sleep or accept new foods as easily as their first child did, or if the younger child is more sensitive, more physically active, or less outgoing than their easier, older child. These parents are not doing anything wrong. Nor is anything wrong with the younger child. His temperament is simply different from that of their "easier" older child.

On the other hand, a child's congenial, agreeable temperament is a powerful factor in building a positive emotional bond between parent and child. Parents who understand the role that temperament plays in a child's life can improve their own parenting abilities and help their child reach a more harmonious fit with situations at home, in school, on the playground, and later in life.

HOW THIS BOOK CAN HELP YOU

Since the mid-1950s, research has been accumulating that sheds clearer light on temperament. As pediatricians, psychiatrists, and psychologists have learned more about temperament, we have acquired a better understanding of its characteristics, how to recognize them in individual children, how to make the most of the positive sides of these traits, and how to help guide the more negative aspects toward a happier outcome.

This book is intended to give parents the benefit of this growing body of research. This is not theory. It is practical, sensible, easily applied information and advice. When temperament is understood correctly, parents can take specific steps to improve the fit between a child's temperament and environment. Here is an example.

The Ferrers' first baby always fell asleep easily and slept through the night regularly. But at eight months of age, their second child does not go to sleep without crying and wakes frequently throughout the night. Her worried, exhausted parents do not understand why this is happening.

"We're doing the same things we did with Luis, but Angela just does not settle down. What are we doing wrong?" they ask themselves, as they warm another bottle in an attempt to quiet her.

The Ferrers need to recognize that Angela simply has a different temperament, one that makes her more sensitive, more irritable, and less easy to soothe than her brother is. They could try an approach to comfort her other than overfeeding her with bottles, which ultimately may lead to excessive weight gain, bottle-mouth dental cavities, or an insufficient intake of solid foods.

The parents cannot change Angela's temperament; however, they can change how they handle her. They could hold her to their shoulder, walk her around a bit before bedtime, rock her, give her a pacifier, darken her bedroom, croon soothing sounds to quiet her restless moments, or let her cry for a few minutes before she drops off to sleep. These activities are more appropriate responses to a baby's sensitive, irritable temperament than giving her more milk. Angela needs more soothing and less stimulation and feeding.

The following chapters explain the nine categories of temperament and how they affect the child, parent, and other caregivers in the child's life. Chapter One defines the nine categories and explains how parents can determine their own child's temperament profile.

For you to obtain the maximum benefit from this book, we ask that you become an active participant by taking notes as you observe the many facets of your child's temperament. This is not a demanding task, and you probably will enjoy it once you have begun. And so, before you read Chapter One, it might be helpful to have a notebook or loose-leaf paper and pencil handy.

A child's temperament is not fully defined by any single trait. Rather, an individual child's temperament is best understood by looking at clusters of traits. Other factors, such as gender, age, intelligence, and development, also come into play. This book explains how these factors make the child's care easier or more difficult.

Common misconceptions often involve age-related behaviors. Many books about child development take a year-by-year approach, for example, implying that all six-year-olds behave identically. Or that all two-year-olds are "terrible." Although certain developmental steps, such as walking and talking, typically occur around a given age, parents should not leap from that fact to an assumption that all three-year-olds will also behave the same way.

Children react to similar situations differently because their temperaments are so individual. Parents should not worry that something is wrong simply because their child does not respond or behave exactly as do other children of the same age, or as her brother did at her age. In this book we discuss temperament from infancy through adolescence; however, we deliberately have not structured this book in chronological order.

Starting with Chapter Three, we discuss how to manage these temperament traits effectively and age-appropriately in a variety of circumstances. Subsequent chapters discuss behavioral problems, developmental issues, physical health, and the role of temperament in school-related problems and crisis situations.

We try to avoid labels in this book. Many parents and professionals focus too heavily on negative behaviors and label children "difficult" or "hyperactive." Yet bothersome behaviors may be normal for a particular child, a part of his or her individual temperament. Although a child's behavior at a particular moment, in a particular setting, may be unacceptable to a parent, that does not indicate that the child is necessarily abnormal.

An understanding and tolerance of a child's temperament does not mean that the child should be given a free ticket to trample other children, shout in class, or otherwise behave inappropriately. It does mean that parents and teachers can learn to recognize certain temperamental characteristics within the child and work with them to reduce the stress and friction they may cause.

A better understanding of temperament can also help parents take a long view: While certain traits may annoy or frustrate them at the moment, those traits can become assets for the child later. A stubborn toddler who is slow to accept new foods, for example, may become a teenager who is less likely to be swayed by peers to try risky behaviors such as experimenting with drugs.

The purpose of this book is not to describe all kinds of behavioral problems but to enrich your understanding of your children's temperaments so that you will be better equipped to prevent and manage problems. Our goal is to help families enjoy greater harmony and appreciate children's unique temperaments, which make them as different as snowflakes.

CHAPTER ONE

Profiling Your Child's Temperament

WHAT TO LOOK FOR AND HOW TO LOOK

This chapter explains the nine categories of temperament and shows you how to identify each. An early warning is needed: This information is not meant to diagnose anything. For now, postpone making judgments about how much you like or dislike these traits in your child, or how you wish to change certain behaviors. Begin by simply reading and thinking about the various characteristics. As you read the descriptions of the nine categories, jot down in a notebook your observations of your child's temperament traits over the past four to six weeks. Using a separate page for each of the nine traits will increase the clarity and organization of your notes. (A sample of one parent's note taking begins on page 24.)

As objectively as you can, watch, listen, and describe the pattern of how your child responds to particular people, settings, and circumstances. Think of this notebook as a journal you might take on a trip. Or, think of yourself as a reporter who does not know this child, as someone who is an impartial, detached, but watchful witness.

The temperament profile will be most accurate if you record your child's behavior in many various settings and at different times. The more samples you collect, the more complete your evaluation will be. For example, observe him when he is watching television, riding in the car, playing alone and with other children, and even while sleeping. Do not only note the occasions when the child is doing things that you dislike or that annoy you, such as running around the house when you are trying to quiet him down before bedtime. What is he doing during quiet, placid times? Does he wiggle around in his bed while he sleeps? Does he fidget when watching a television program that is relatively calm, for example, *Mister Rogers Neighborhood* or *Barney*, as opposed to an action-adventure movie? Observe him when he is in new, unfamiliar surroundings as well as when he is eating, dressing, meeting people, or reacting to a surprise or a disappointment. Write down any other relevant factors in your journal: Is this particular behavior typical or not?

As you observe your child, it will probably become apparent very quickly that some temperament traits are easier to spot than others. In the sensitivity category, for example, your child may make your observational task easy by showing you repeatedly and consistently that she is sensitive to soft sounds, changes in lighting, rough-textured clothing, and even the subtlest changes in room temperature. In another area, such as adaptability, it may be more difficult to assess her reactions. She may seem to adapt smoothly to some situations but not others, and therefore you may have more difficulty in determining her adaptability trait.

If it is not immediately clear how your child functions in any one of these nine areas, you may want to take more extensive notes about observations in those areas over a longer period of time and in a greater variety of settings. The more uncertain you are about a particular temperament trait, the more important it is to keep detailed notes. In this way, your conclusions will be more accurate and meaningful.

It may seem too time-consuming for busy parents to take notes about their children's reactions in various environments. Or some parents may believe that they already know their child's temperament well enough. The rewarding result of writing down your detached observations, however, can be an improved perspective about your child. It may also help to identify some concerns that have been overlooked. Hastily or superficially formed impressions of a child's behavior, whether by parents or professionals, are sometimes correct but are very likely to be incomplete or biased by expectations and preferences. Try to avoid snap judgments.

It is highly important to use descriptive terms and avoid negative labels such as "obnoxious," "wild," "demanding," "insecure," "immature," "jumpy," "lazy," and so forth. Each of these can be replaced by a neutral or even positive description, such as the following:

> *Energetic* instead of *hyper*
>
> *Cautious* instead of *timid*
>
> *Assertive* instead of *stubborn*
>
> *Perceptive* instead of *overly sensitive*
>
> *Enthusiastic* instead of *loud*
>
> *Dramatic* instead of *explosive*

Some of the behaviors you want to describe may not be temperament traits at all and will not fit into these categories. They may be behavioral adjustment issues such as poor self-esteem, aggressiveness, or uncooperative behavior. These issues are discussed in Chapter Four. Be sure to write them down, too—but on a separate page in your notebook—if they do not seem to belong in one of the nine categories. If you have concerns that some of your child's behaviors may be influenced by physical factors such as reactions to certain foods, you should discuss this possibility with your child's pediatrician or your family physician.

As your notebook fills up, you will probably begin to notice patterns in the way your child reacts to certain environments, stimuli, and situations. At this point, you will be ready to move on to Chapter Two, in which we discuss how your tolerance and intolerance of these various traits affect both your child and you. In Chapter Three, we suggest ways of managing these temperament traits. Be patient. It is better first to understand temperament before starting to manage it.

NINEPATCHES

Amish women have a common quilt design that is at least a century old. It is the simplest pattern, the one a mother uses to teach her daughters the craft of quilting. Called a ninepatch, it is composed of three squares over three, over three more. Each square has its own texture and color. Imagine this example: purple, light green, brown, bright blue, red, gray, mauve, magenta, pale yellow. A dark patch is arranged next to a lighter one until a tic-tac-toe design comes together. Each square relates to the one next to it and to the quilt pattern as a whole.

When researchers started to examine human temperament about forty years ago, they were not thinking about quilts. But the comparison is useful. Beginning with the groundbreaking work of Chess and Thomas, researchers have identified nine categories of largely inborn temperament that help us understand how children experience and react to their environments. These nine patches of different temperament colors and materials can be arranged to form many kinds of designs, sometimes orderly, sometimes overlapping and irregular, but always unique.

Some temperament traits are more evident in certain settings than they are in others, just as a vivid red patch might attract your eye more than an adjacent gray patch would. As you read about these traits, observe how they reveal themselves in the situations described. Your main aims should be to describe and rate, which may require a bit of comparison with other children of the same age. If this is your first child, if you do not know many children of the same age as your child, or if it is difficult to make objective observations of your child, you may want to enlist someone else in helping you make these observations—your spouse, friends, relatives, day care worker, or schoolteacher. Whomever you choose should know your child, and children in general, fairly well.

If your children are teenagers, you may want to invite them to participate in assessing their own temperaments. They are probably mature enough to share this exercise and may contribute information that you might not otherwise have. (For more about teenagers, see page 21.)

All nine traits are present in children to varying degrees. In any given child, each trait may run from very high to somewhat high, to average, to somewhat low, to very low. After you have read the following descriptions of each trait, decide where you think your child should be placed within the range of each trait. Then write your conclusions in your notebook.

ACTIVITY

The activity characteristic of temperament refers to physical motion during sleep, play, work, eating, dressing, bathing, and other daily circumstances. Look at your child's spontaneous activity. Does she bounce about from one foot to another while she is waiting for school bus to arrive? Does he crawl all over the house during most of his waking hours? Does she wiggle about in the crib or on the changing table? Or, does he move through daily activities more like the tortoise than the hare, at a slower, steady tempo?

Look also at nonspontaneous, or reactive, activity. How much motion does your child exhibit in response to people and situations? When you walk through the doorway after a long day at work, does your toddler race toward you, walk slowly to you, or wait for you to come to her? When he is tired or hungry, what is his physical response? Is he whirling in motion, hopping or running about, swinging his arms or kicking his legs? Or does he curl up, sit quietly, and wait for sleep or food to arrive?

As you watch your child's physical motion in different settings, look for patterns in play. Children who are very active generally enjoy bouncing, jumping, running, and tumbling. Less active children prefer less vigorous games and sports. As toddlers, they do not enjoy bouncing on Grandpa's knee for a "horsy ride." As kindergartners, they do not care to climb up and down the jungle gym or attempt the see-saw. Children who are less active may prefer to turn the rope rather than jump it. For a teenager, consider the choice of sports activities: cross-country running or archery, for example.

Look at how much vigorous motion and how much inactivity, or low motion, your child exhibits during feedings or mealtime. Watch your child's amount of motion as she eats. Does the baby or toddler generally sit still? Or, does she squirm or try to climb out of the high chair as she is being fed? When the older child eats at the table, does he tap the chair legs with his feet throughout the meal or fiddle nonstop with his utensils?

During daily procedures, such as diapering, bathing, hair brushing, and dressing, how active or immobile is the child? How much does the baby splash and kick in the bathtub? How much does he move about when you are trying to dress him? This is most easily seen in infants and toddlers but also can be observed in older children. For example, as she brushes her teeth, does she stand still at the sink, or does she parade around the bathroom or hop up and down in front of the mirror?

Watch young children in their car seats and strollers. How active are they in those harnessed environments? Watch them when they are crying. Do they thrash about or sob without much physical movement? Watch them when they are alone. Do they choose low-motion activities such as board games, reading, and drawing, or do they prefer riding a bike or rollerblading?

Observe them in different social circumstances and gauge the degree of their physical motion during these times: when they are alone with you; when they are with other children; and when they are watching television, reading, or doing homework. How still or active are they?

Look also at their activity levels in unfamiliar settings. How physically active are they when exploring new turf? If you are visiting a neighbor's home, where your toddler has never been before, does he explore the kitchen and open every drawer and cabinet door? Or, does he sit still on your lap, content to play with a toy or look at a book that you have brought along? On visiting day at a new summer camp, does your ten-year-old run from soccer field to cabin to lake, scoping out the whole scene, or does he saunter along behind the tour guide from place to place?

After you have observed your child's physical motion in different places over a period of time, would you say that this child is highly active? Does she have an average, or a mix, of activity levels? Or is her physical motion generally low in most circumstances? Jot down these observations in your notebook; they will be useful later. The more you write down now about this characteristic and the others that follow, the more accurate will be your overall assessment of your child's functioning.

REGULARITY

This trait refers to the predictable recurrence of a child's responses to the events in her daily life. In young children, regularity is most easily observed in the rhythm of their bodily processes and functions, such as sleeping, eating, and elimination. As children move into the elementary school years, regularity is better observed as consistency, organization, or predictable patterns of their social behavior, such as completing tasks on schedule. Let's look first at younger children.

As a baby, she is fairly predictable in bodily functions. She gets hungry at regular times and sucks for about the same amount of time at each feeding. Nearly every day, she falls asleep around the same hour for naps and bedtime. She sleeps the same number of hours each night and wakes about the same time every morning. Her bowel movements occur regularly. She is fussy and most active at certain times of the day. This is a child who seems to have an inner clock telling her to operate on schedule. Less regular infants keep parents guessing about when they will be hungry and sleepy. It will be harder to get these babies onto an organized schedule.

As an older child, the regular youngster eats about equal amounts of food at all meals and snacks in a fairly routine pattern every afternoon after school. With older children, however, parents are usually less aware of the details or occurrence of these daily bodily rhythms, and therefore it is not as easy to rate regularity by the same criteria as it is with very young children. Instead, consider the predictability of the school-age child's personal habits and organization. Is she orderly about her toys, clothes, and room? Is the after-school routine about the same each day; for example, does she come in, grab a snack, and run back outside to play on a regular basis? Or is each day a surprise? Does she do her household chores and homework about the same time every day? Does she seem to enjoy a predictable routine to daily life?

In observing your child's rhythms, consider a range of settings and events over time and try to decide if the child is predominantly regular and predictable, like clockwork, or if his reactions and activities are difficult to anticipate. Or is he somewhere in between regularity and unpredictability?

INITIAL REACTION

For this category, observe how your child responds to new stimuli. What is his initial reaction to new people, situations, places, foods, toys, and procedures? Your observations will gauge how bold or hesitant your child is when faced with unfamiliar, novel environments.

When a new babysitter arrives, does your child seem at ease and willing to show her his bedroom and playthings? Or is he withdrawn and shy? Watch how he approaches other new people: a new teacher or new doctor, or visitors to your home, new children he meets on the playground, strangers in the supermarket who comment about how adorable he is.

A distinction must be made between a typical, established reaction pattern and a specific avoidance behavior based on an unfavorable experience, such as a child's staying away from dogs after being bitten or avoiding unfamiliar people if he has been mistreated.

Recall Michael from the Introduction. Does your child also wait on the sidelines and warm up slowly in a new day care setting, classroom, or playground? Does she take her time to engage in new activities or games with other children? In many different situations, watch how your child reacts to novelty. Does he accept it and jump right in, or does he hesitate or pull back?

As you make these observations, watch for the numerous mundane yet still new experiences in your child's life, not just the major events such as starting a new school or moving to a new home.

Look at the child's reaction to different foods, both those never before tasted and familiar foods served in new ways. Does she agree to taste a peanut butter and banana sandwich when all she has eaten previously is peanut butter and jelly? If he is used to raw carrots, will he accept cooked ones? If you run out of her favorite cereals, will she be willing to try some unfamiliar ones? When he is at a friend's house and the brand of juice is different from what he is used to at home, will he drink it?

When you make these observations about foods, note whether your child initially accepted or rejected the new food. Did she try it? Did she immediately refuse to eat it? Or did she look it over, poke at it, and gradually decide to taste a bite? The point of these observations is not to record how much new food a child will eat or whether she ultimately accepts it, but to note her initial reaction pattern to novel, unfamiliar foods.

Look for patterns of response also when your child is confronted with a wide variety of new situations at home, in school, and in the community. How does he react when a new task is introduced at home or in school? For the latter situations, teachers can help by contributing their observations.

When you visit a relative or friend's home, how does the child respond to an unfamiliar physical environment, for example, sleeping in a new bed or bathing in a different bathtub? Try to determine where your child is on a range between bold and inhibited in initial responses. At one end of this range is the child who accepts and approaches ordinary degrees of novelty with little hesitation or plunges in quickly. At the other end is the shy or timid child who does not engage in new situations or withdraws from them entirely, at least for a while. Most children, of course, are in the middle of this range.

ADAPTABILITY

This quality is related to but should not be confused with the "initial reaction" category described previously. Adaptability is the longer-term adjustment that follows the initial response. Adaptability refers to the ease or difficulty with which a child's first reaction can be changed in a socially desirable way. It shows a range between flexibility and rigidity in adjusting to the environment after the initial response has occurred. A positive initial reaction and high adaptability—or their opposites—tend to go together, but not necessarily.

Again, recall Michael. He can be described as "slow to warm up" or shy in his initial response to new situations such as his day care setting. Michael is also slowly adaptable. Several days and weeks later, he still needed coaxing to get him involved in group activities. A more adaptable child might take only a day or two.

When observing your child's adaptability, watch how rapidly or slowly she makes the transition—after her initial response—from an established pattern of behavior to a reasonable, new requirement by teacher, day care worker, babysitter, you, or your spouse. For example, relatives will be visiting for the weekend and your eight-year-old must not only give up her bedroom to Grandma and sleep in a sleeping bag in the baby's room, but she also must take her bath and get ready for bed earlier than usual to accommodate everyone else in the household.

She does not particularly like this turn of events, but watch how she adapts. Does she try to postpone the inevitable by talking you into another plan, by dawdling as she gathers her night clothes and sleeping bag, or by other delaying tactics? Or does she say, "Okay, good night" and accept the new arrangement quickly?

With a younger child, the adaptability trait can be observed in a variety of everyday procedures: When a babysitter is supposed to feed, bathe, and put the child to bed, does she put up much resistance? Does she cooperate when there is a change of routine with diapering, hair brushing, face washing, or nail cutting? If Mom usually oversees the evening bath, how does the child react when Dad pinch-hits and has a different routine? Does the child fight the change with protests such as "Mommy always lets me play with my bath toys longer before I have to be rinsed"? Or does she adapt readily to Dad's brisker soap, rinse, towel-off pace?

Observe play situations. When another child or several children join an ongoing activity, does your child accept a new playmate easily, or does he resist? Does he demand that the game stop, take his marbles, and go home? Or does he continue with the activity and include the new players? How does he accept other children's rules for playing the game?

Look also at how quickly your child makes decisions. Offered choices between playing one of two favorite games, or between visiting one friend or another, does she have difficulty making up her mind? Does she choose one rapidly and decisively, with the realization that both would be fun but since she cannot do both simultaneously, one is better than none? Or does she agonize over the choice, procrastinate about making a decision, and fight the notion that she cannot do both?

Another good situation for evaluating adaptability is when family plans must change at the last moment, for example, when rain has canceled a camping trip or ball game. Does your child accept the circumstances fairly easily despite his disappointment, or does he dig in his heels and plead, "Why can't we go anyway?"

As you observe your child's adaptability in different settings, ask yourself if she adapting with relative ease to normal changes in circumstances and to established necessities, such as face washing. Does she have trouble accepting reasonable changes? Is she inflexible? Or is she average, somewhere in between rigidity and flexibility?

INTENSITY

Intensity is the measure of how much energy your child puts into his responses. Recall Suzannah from the Introduction. She is an intense child who responds vigorously, with a loud voice and physical activity. A milder, placid child reacts with little expression of feeling, vocalization, or physical motion.

Intensity refers to the amount of energy in the child's response, regardless of whether it is positive and happy or negative and fussy. An intense child both laughs and cries loudly. A milder child just smiles and whimpers.

Watch for intensity in a various situations. Is it explosive or gentle? Loud or soft? A young child expresses degrees of intensity during most waking moments: when hungry, full, and tired; when a food is enjoyed or disliked; when a diaper is wet or soiled; while being changed, bathed, or dressed; and when feeling pain. Also observe the young child's reaction to other kinds of stimulation, such as tickling, bright lights, and music.

Observe the strength of the child's responses to both new and familiar people, whether positive or negative. Also consider his response to discipline, that is, whether he is intense or mild in acceptance or noncompliance. A less intense child may whine, whereas a more intense child may raise his voice in reaction to a disciplinary measure.

As children grow older, you can observe the intensity of their reactions to all kinds of likes and dislikes. Watch, for instance, how intense their reactions may be to praise, failure, surprise, frustration, new toys and games, or interruption of their play activities.

In appraising your child's overall intensity trait, consider many situations and determine if your child's reaction is generally intense, average, or mild. Observations of other children are particularly helpful here to give you a basis for comparison.

MOOD

Every child displays a variety of emotional moments: happy and sad, cheery and glum, cuddly and grumpy. In assessing your child's predisposition for mood, look for an overall pattern—a thread woven through many different situations—to determine whether the child's predominant mood is positive, negative, or somewhere in between.

Note instances of pleasant, friendly behavior and of unpleasant, unfriendly behavior in various circumstances. The child with a positive mood smiles often and spontaneously, laughs a lot, and is friendly with most people; in other words, he has a sunny, upbeat disposition. A child with a negative mood trait reacts with unpleasant, unfriendly responses; he is fussy, complaining, and less amiable around other people.

Mood is apparent throughout the day. Consider your child's mood when she is waking and going to sleep; before, during, and after meals; when having a bowel movement (if she is very young); and during daily routines such as bathing, face and hand washing, hair brushing, and dressing. Also observe her mood when new clothes are tried on, when a visitor is introduced, when greeting familiar people, while playing, and when the child is alone.

Notice your child's mood when she is sick or injured, while being examined by the doctor, and when siblings are around. With older children, look at mood as it is expressed during playtime with other children, events at school, birthday parties, and in response to requests for help with household chores.

If your child is a teenager, you can expect wide swings in mood, from gaiety one moment to the blues the next. Mood swings are normal for teenagers. By adolescence you should know your child well enough to determine whether his predominant mood tends to be generally sunny or generally glum.

After making many observations in different circumstances, you can now decide how your child's overall mood compares with other children you know.

PERSISTENCE AND ATTENTION SPAN

Persistence refers to the child's tendency to stick with the activity despite obstacles or interruptions of all sorts, for example, sounds from outdoors, background noise from the radio or television, and the movement of other children milling about the room. Attention span is demonstrated by how long a child sticks to an activity or pursues a task when there are no interruptions.

Persistence is similar to attention span and differs only as to the impact of the interruption. The two traits are grouped together here because they are interrelated. Although some very attentive children may be more easily disrupted by what is going on around them than others are, they are usually persistent and promptly return to what they were doing.

A child with low persistence and a short attention span focuses on schoolwork or a play activity for only a short time. The child with greater persistence and a longer attention span concentrates on the activity at hand, largely ignoring surrounding distractions, interruptions, and obstacles. When distracted, he may look up from what he is doing but quickly returns to it.

Of course, it is not easy to pinpoint these qualities in a very young infant. However, an estimate can be made based on how long the baby watches people and things in the immediate surroundings. Older infants and toddlers exhibit persistence and attention span while they play with toys and explore their environments. A very persistent toddler will pull and poke and fiddle with the knobs on a cabinet door until he unlatches it. A less persistent one will more likely move on to something else after his first a · empt at opening the door has failed. As children become older, you can observe these traits in many other ways. With what degree of attention and persistence does your child listen to your instructions, perform both easy and difficult household tasks, read, do homework, and practice sports skills or musical instruments? As you are certainly aware, attention span increases with age.

Once again, observe your child in many settings and determine where your child stands within this range. Is she highly attentive and persistent, somewhere in the middle, or unlikely to stay with an activity very long?

DISTRACTIBILITY

Is your child easily distracted by stimuli around her? Or does she usually tune out surrounding sights, sounds, lights, or people and continue whatever she is doing without interruption?

Distractibility is not the opposite of persistence because a child can be very easily distracted yet still return immediately to the task at hand and stick with it until it is finished. That child would be considered high in distractibility but also high in persistence. (The senior author acknowledges this combination of traits in himself.)

In babies, distractibility is measured mainly by how quickly and easily they can be soothed. How easily can you calm your infant with a distraction—for example, shaking a rattle, cooing, rocking, rubbing his back, gently stroking an arm or leg—when he is hungry; tired; frightened; in pain; in need of a diaper change; or uncomfortable during bathing, dressing, or hair brushing? An easily distracted baby in some discomfort can be soothed more quickly and easily than can a less distractible baby.

Distractibility in older children is observed by watching how they respond to outside stimuli. Is the child easily sidetracked by disturbances or interruptions during meals? If someone walks into the kitchen while she is eating breakfast, does she look up and stop eating? When reading or doing homework, is he distracted by the sound of a distant fire siren? While doing household tasks, such as putting away toys and clothes, does he stop what he is doing if the cat romps across his path? How easily is she sidetracked by interrupting stimuli when playing with her friends or with favorite games and toys?

To determine the distractibility trait of your child's temperament, look for a predominant pattern in the child's response to interruptions and distractions. How easily is the baby soothed by a caregiver or the older child's attention deflected by outside interference? Is she likely to continue whatever she has been doing despite the stimulus, or is she easily distracted? Or does she fall somewhere in the middle, exhibiting a mixture of both kinds of responses?

SENSITIVITY

Sensitivity refers to a child's sensory threshold, or the amount of stimulation from outside factors—such as noises, sights, smells, and lights—needed to rouse a response. This is not the same trait as distractibility, which refers to whether stimuli interfere with the child's behavior or what he is doing at that given moment. Sensitivity refers to the child's awareness of that stimulus as shown by any response, even a brief one.

Through their behavior, highly sensitive children reveal that they are sharply aware of their environment. Less sensitive children are less aware of, and therefore less responsive to the same stimuli.

All five senses give clues to the child's sensitivity trait. Watch to see how your child responds to visual cues, such as changes in room lighting or, perhaps, a change in a familiar person's physical appearance. If she selects her own clothing, does she notice subtle color or texture differences?

With regard to hearing, how aware is he of soft sounds? How does he respond to loud noises? Sounds in the next room? Music drifting down from upstairs? A slight increase in the television volume?

With regard to touch, how does he react to tight or itchy clothing? Does he comment on the feel of ordinary clothing? Does he reject shirts with collars or turtlenecks and prefer loose crew necks? How does the baby react to wet or soiled diapers? Temperature of the bath water? Dirt on his knees? Bumps during a car ride? Does he notice a soft breeze from the window?

With regard to smell, does she seem to notice the aroma of particular foods more or less than others? The smells of someone else's home when visiting? Does she show awareness of the odor of a new car's interior? The lingering fragrance of an air freshener? Outdoor smells when riding in a car or bus with open windows?

Taste is one of the easiest senses to observe in children. How does he react to foods with both strong and mild flavors? If he is used to salted or seasoned foods, does he notice if those seasonings are omitted? Does she comment on the flavor of a new toothpaste if you switch brands?

Again, in making your observations, look for a predominant pattern and try to determine how sensitive your child is. Is this a child who is acutely aware of, and responsive to, sensory stimuli inside and outside his body? Is the child fairly average in sensory responses? Or does it take a greater amount of stimuli to jolt a response from this child? There may be greater sensitivity in some areas, such as taste, and less in others, such as hearing.

Differences in social sensitivity become observable as children become older. They may display different responses to changes in a familiar person's clothing or hairstyle or to various sorts of people, male or female, old or young, with or without glasses or beards.

With increasing maturity, children display different amounts of awareness of and sensitivity to the thoughts and feelings of others. For example, with varying degrees of accuracy, children become able to perceive and interpret subtle changes in tone of voice and facial expressions. Sensitivity to the thoughts and feelings of others is difficult to observe and rate in younger children.

CLUSTERING OF TRAITS

In any child, no single trait defines the whole temperament. All nine traits are present in every child, although some appear to be more dominant than others. Each category has its own identity, yet it relates to the others. Temperament is formed by a mixture of elements. As with the ninepatch quilt, it is important to look both at the overall pattern and the individual patches.

Some of these categories tend to cluster together, much like the dark and light hues of the quilt. Many shy children, for example, typically exhibit a combination of the following five traits: slow initial response, more difficulty modifying their reactions in a desirable way (adaptability), lower energy levels of response (intensity), less physical activity, and a more negative mood.

Thomas and Chess originally introduced the cluster of difficult temperament consisting of timidity in initial reactions, slow adaptability, high intensity, predominantly negative mood, and irregularity. Although the term *difficult* has become popular, and many find it convenient, the danger of misuse and misunderstanding makes us reluctant to encourage its use. It can also be a disparaging term that may lead adults to look for or expect all kinds of so-called difficulty from a child.

The term *easy* for the opposite of the difficult traits is more understandable and acceptable. The easy cluster usually describes children who are pleasant, flexible, not too intense, and fairly predictable. Other clusters are discussed in Chapter Seven.

SPECIAL CONSIDERATIONS FOR NEWBORNS

We have heard many parents of older children and young adults make observations such as the following: "His temperament has not changed since the day he was born." Or "My two daughters have such very different temperaments, and those differences have been apparent in each one since birth."

Although these reflections may be true, we do not recommend trying to estimate your infant's temperament in the first several weeks of life. The main reason is that, although newborn babies do show significant behavioral individuality, these differences appear at present to be predominantly a reflection of temporary influences during pregnancy and delivery, such as maternal health and diet, duration of labor, and type of obstetrical anesthesia. These differences are not the largely genetically determined ones that will emerge during the next few weeks. Many of the variations mentioned earlier in this chapter, such as initial reaction and adaptation to new people and foods, simply are not observable in a newborn.

When parents gaze at the newborn baby in their arms, they may wonder which traits they can observe and how long lasting they will be. Scientists and clinicians who study newborn behavior speak of differences in state and differences in trait. At any given moment a baby can be rated as to his or her state, which ranges from deep sleep to active sleep, to drowsiness, to quiet alert, to active alert, to crying. But that is about as far as we can go in describing the qualities of behavior in newborns. All newborns show all of these states.

The newborn's traits are the amounts and patterns of the states that the baby shows; that is, how sleepy, irritable, easily aroused, or soothed the baby is. A small amount of continuity of some of these traits over time has been demonstrated but only over the course of a few months at most.

It has been said that a newborn's behavior is more like the preface of a book than the table of contents. Behavioral scientists have shown that individual behavioral differences in newborns are not particularly lasting. This makes predictions from the newborn period unlikely to be accurate. It also means that if a newborn baby has certain characteristics that are not to your liking, such as completely irregular feeding and sleeping patterns, there is a good chance the problem will improve before long. By three or four months at the latest, temperament has started to show significant stability, which increases for the next few years and probably continues into adolescence.

Parents of premature infants often ask whether their child's temperament differs from that of a full-term baby. About six percent of babies in the United States are born prematurely and weigh less than five and a half pounds. At first, they are different in some ways. Generally, they are less active and less alert, have shorter sleep periods, are harder to soothe, and have higher-pitched cries. After discharge from the hospital, premature babies have been described as typically being more irritable, less responsive to stimuli, and irregular in their sleep and feeding patterns.

Current reports indicate that most of these differences disappear over the first few months of life for most of these low-birth-weight infants. However, we cannot say when and how this happens. If a prematurely born baby is extremely small, and especially if there has been bleeding in the brain, the chances of some of these differences persisting seem to be greater. Surveys of temperament characteristics of physically normal premature infants from six months of age on show that by that age, they have the same range of traits as do full-term babies. In other words, these early differences appear to be only temporary for most premature infants.

Babies who are small for their gestational age (SGA) are even smaller than they should be for their degree of prematurity. Research evidence is mixed about whether this SGA subgroup of premature babies has additional or different temperament variations. The uncertainty probably stems from the fact that their smaller size has various causes, such as diseases in the mother or child or pregnancy problems, with diverse effects.

SPECIAL CONCERNS WITH ADOLESCENTS

Teenagers are another special case. Most temperament assessments rely on parents' observations and reporting, as we have done in this chapter. Adolescents, however, are able to report on themselves and may insist on doing so. Should you use your observations or those of your teenager? Why not use both? As a parent, you are able to describe the behavior with greater objectivity and with a far greater background of experience. But only the teenager knows how she or he really feels.

An adolescent who was very shy as a young child, for example, may no longer *appear* to feel uncomfortable in new situations, because he has learned to push himself forward when it is required of him. Yet he may still *feel* shy inwardly. How should his temperament be described and rated? Ideally, your judgments of your teenager's temperament should combine his observations and yours.

Your teenager may show no interest whatsoever in assessing his or her temperament. Some teenagers may even think such an exercise is an invasion of their privacy. If that is so, do not insist. You can make your own observations. If you want to try to involve your teenager in a discussion of temperament, it is probably better to do so informally during a noncrisis time, rather than during a heated moment. If a teenager's temperament trait—such as low persistence and short attention span—bothers the parent, it will not be helpful to raise the subject of temperament assessment in the middle of a confrontation over poor grades on the report card. The teenager would probably be more receptive during a quieter time when there is no immediate problem at hand.

Some parents have found that leaving a book such as this one on the kitchen table invites an adolescent to pick it up and browse through it casually. The parent might say something such as, "I've been reading about how kids have different temperaments, and I thought I'd try to profile your little sister's temperament. Would you be interested in doing your own, too?" If your teenager is not interested, the subject can be dropped. You may discover that some teenagers, being naturally introspective and curious, may later revisit the subject to learn more about their own temperaments or those of their siblings or friends.

With all the changes—physiological, emotional, cognitive—that accompany adolescence, parents often wonder about the role that temperament plays during these years. Despite a shortage of research studies that follow children's temperament differences into adolescence, we have every reason to believe that an individual's temperament continues with a fair degree of stability into the teenage years and beyond.

We can continue to think of temperament in the same nine dimensions as we have during the earlier years; however, during adolescence—from about age 11 or 12 through age 18 or 21—some new factors may contribute to and influence a young person's temperament. These include normal sex hormones, dietary eccentricities, sleep deprivation, rigorous athletic training, and use of substances such as drugs, alcohol, and tobacco.

By adolescence a child may have become quite competent at altering the expression of his temperament, especially if it becomes evident to him that doing so will help him to get along better with people, in school, or at a job. Curbing intensity or pushing oneself forward despite feeling timid, for example, may improve the "fit" in the increasingly complex world of adolescence, even though the teenager still feels the intensity or the shyness internally. Does this mean that the temperament has changed? Yes and no. Although the expression may be different, it is likely that the feelings are still there.

Parents frequently wonder whether and how temperament affects the nature and duration of teenage rebellion. Adolescence is almost always stressful but only sometimes stormy. Informal observations indicate that a child's temperament is an important factor in determining whether the normal passage through these years is rough or smooth. Traits such as adaptability and mood undoubtedly continue to matter. In addition to temperament characteristics, such factors as parental guidance and extrafamilial social influences are equally powerful in affecting how smooth or choppy a teenager's passage through adolescence will be.

BEFORE YOU GO ON

By now you should have a notebook full of observations and ratings of all nine temperament traits as seen in your child's behavior over a period of time and in many different settings. To show you how another parent profiled her son's temperament characteristics, a sample follows at the end of this chapter. It is included only to offer an example of this exercise in observation and rating. Keep in mind that your style of note-taking may differ and that your child may be quite different from Teddy, the four-and-a-half-year-old in the sample. But your goal is the same: Make as many detailed observations as you can because, when taken together, they will paint a more comprehensive portrait of your child's temperament.

It also may be helpful if you show your notes to someone else who knows your child well—a relative, friend, or teacher. That person may wish to make a separate list of observations to compare with yours or may simply review your notes to see how much general agreement you both have about the child's traits. When in doubt, trust your own observations, because you are the expert on your child.

Please remember not to make judgments about how much you enjoy or dislike any of these traits or about how they affect your relationship with your child. Hold those thoughts for the next chapter.

OBSERVATIONS OF TEDDY, AGED 4 YEARS, 6 MONTHS

After observing Teddy's reactions in a wide variety of situations over time, his parents concluded that their son has a mixture of highs, lows, and averages in the nine temperament dimensions. This is a fairly typical pattern, as many parents discover when they first profile a child's temperament. As they look more closely at the individual traits, parents can then decide which areas are of most concern to them and which need attention to improve the "fit." These matters are discussed in Chapters Two and Three.

ACTIVITY

Sleep   Lies fairly still when sleeping at night or while napping during the day. When I go in to check on him before I go to bed and in the morning before he awakes, he is usually in the same position as when I tucked him in at bedtime. Occasionally thrashes around some during the first hour or two if he has been really upset about something earlier in the day.

Play   Teddy likes many kinds of games, but mostly quiet, indoor ones and those he can play by himself: coloring, looking at picture books, listening to music. While watching TV and being read to, he sits still and does not squirm. When we are out walking, he stays with us and does not dash off ahead.

Work   He does not have many chores, but those he does, such as carrying his dishes to the sink after meals, are carried out slowly.

Eating   Eats slowly and steadily. He is not one to be bouncing out of his chair every two minutes like some other children. When we went out to a restaurant Sunday, he sat where we asked him, even though he complained a bit about the location. While waiting for the food to arrive, he sat in his seat and did not try to get up and wander around.

Dressing   Mostly dresses himself, but does it slowly, especially with his shoes and socks. His older brother and younger sister could dress themselves in half the time it takes him. When he needs help, as with pulling a shirt over his head or starting a zipper, he usually holds fairly still. This makes it easier for me than it was with his brother at the same age.

Bathing   Plays quietly with plastic boats and ducks in the tub. Sometimes he makes noises or sings to himself, but hardly splashes at all. No need to worry about mopping up a flooded floor after his bath!

Places   We visited a shoe store earlier this week, and later we stopped by my friend's house. Even after he had been there for a while, he did not run around to explore in either place.

Activity rating   I would say Teddy is a relatively inactive child, not because he cannot get up speed, but because he simply prefers to operate slowly.

REGULARITY

Eating   Fairly regular as to when he gets hungry; seems to be ready to eat something at mealtimes, but is not so predictable when it comes to the amount of food he eats. Some days, he cleans his plate and asks for more. Other days, he takes just a few bites and then picks at the rest of his food. His interest in a morning or afternoon snack (time, type, amount) is quite unpredictable.

Sleep   When he feels sleepy at night varies by as much as an hour or two from one night to the next. But he always wakes up at about the same time (7 A.M.), on weekdays and weekends.

Bowel habits   Very regular. Every morning right after breakfast, he goes off to the bathroom. He has been this way for a long time.

Energy   Teddy is not a highly active child, but it seems his spurts of greatest energy vary somewhat from day to day. Yesterday, for example, he seemed more energetic than I had noticed in the past week. On some days, he wants to go outside to play in the morning. On other days, he prefers the afternoon.

Regularity rating   Teddy seems to be a mixture of regularity and irregularity. Overall, I guess he is average.

INITIAL REACTION

New people, adults   Teddy was slow to warm up to the last two babysitters. Unlike his brother and sister, he stayed upstairs and peered at the babysitters through the railing for about 20 minutes before coming downstairs to say hello. He almost never talks to an

(continued)

unfamiliar adult, whether in a store, at a neighborhood gathering, or at our own house, until he has hung out with them for at least 20 or 30 minutes.

New people, other children   Shy with new children. Hides behind me and will not talk to unfamiliar children at first, at least until the other child makes an overture to him such as showing him a toy or game.

New places   These are a challenge for Ted. When he started day-care last fall, he did not want to go and did not want me to leave him there. It took three weeks before he would let me just take him to the door and leave without staying awhile.

Even though he is fascinated by animals, he did not want to go to the zoo at first, not until he learned that two friends would be going, too. When we visited his grandparents at their new house last month, he had trouble getting used to the different bed and bathroom.

We went to a new park last week in which the climbing equipment and swings were very different from our neighborhood playground. His sister and brother immediately raced around, trying out one thing and then the next. Teddy walked around and looked over everything before testing a sliding board, first taking his own sweet time getting used to the new scene. After about an hour, he was enjoying himself so much that did not want to come home.

New situations   When we got a new television a few days ago, we rearranged the furniture in the living room. His brother and sister hardly paid any attention to the new plan, but Teddy still keeps telling us that the sofa belongs back where it was before.

New foods   No new ones this week. Teddy will usually accept new foods, except for vegetables, although he is likely to refuse them the first few times I offer them.

New clothes   Whenever I buy him something new, such as shoes or a shirt, he lets it sit around for a few days before he will try it on and wear it. He seems to like his old clothes best.

New procedures   No new ones in the past few weeks.

New toys   Generally does not start to play with them immediately. When he got a new bike for his birthday, he looked it over very carefully for several minutes instead of jumping right on and trying it out. When he finally got on, he was beaming and really enjoyed it.

Initial reaction rating   Teddy shows a consistent picture of hesitation, inhibition, shyness, or withdrawal in initial reactions.

ADAPTABILITY

With adults   He takes a while to adjust to new adults in his life. The new barber, for example. Even after his third haircut, Teddy hardly spoke to him, although the man was very pleasant and tried to make Ted feel comfortable. "He doesn't cut my hair like Mr. D. used to," he complained to me on the way home.

Teddy also still hides when the new mail carrier comes to the door. He asks, "Where is the man who used to bring our letters? I don't like this new mailman."

With children   They take time, too. He still avoids the little boy who moved in next door about six weeks ago. "He's not my friend," Teddy says when I suggest that he play with him. (Since they are about the same age, I was hoping they would become good buddies.) When he plays with other children, Teddy usually tries to get them to go by his rules, The day-care teacher also mentioned this tendency.

Places   On Tuesday he brought home a permission slip from daycare for a group trip to a fire station, but he said he did not want to go. By the next day, he had changed his mind and told me that his pal Sam wants to see the inside of a firehouse and climb on a ladder truck; Sam has apparently persuaded Ted to come along.

Foods   Acceptance of new foods takes time; no new ones tried in the last two or three weeks. Still dislikes most vegetables.

Clothes   His big brother offered Teddy his old shirt. At first, Teddy rejected it but later seemed glad to have it and put it on, probably because he admires his brother and tries to be like him.

Household rules and discipline   It is tough to get Teddy to comply with rules. It is hard to coax him out of forbidden activities and to get him to accept limitations on his activities, such as when it is time to finish something and come to the table or take his bath. He eventually adjusts to the rules, but it takes him longer than it did

(continued)

his brother when he was his age and, I think, with most children his own age. We are trying to be firm and consistent so he understands we mean business. Fortunately, no changes in household rules in the last couple of weeks. We are trying to keep changes to a minimum because he has such a problem adjusting to them.

Change in plans   He got very upset last weekend when his father was unable to take him for their usual Saturday morning outing to play in the park. A typical reaction for him.

Acceptance of established personal routines (face and hand washing before eating, brushing teeth, and so on)   He used to fuss during all these activities but has been tolerating them better over the past two months. He still protests about getting his nails cut, though.

Adaptability rating   Teddy is generally slow to adapt to changes and to established requirements.

INTENSITY

Sensory stimulation   Although he squeals with delight when we tickle him, he generally does not startle or react very much to loud noises or bright lights.

Hunger   As a baby, he only whimpered when hungry. Since he has been able to talk, he just tells us quietly when he is hungry.

Being full   Similarly, when he is full, he just stops eating and declines more food. No loud refusals.

Need to urinate or have bowel movement   He just saunters off to the toilet by himself without a big commotion.

Food   When he likes or dislikes a food, he simply smiles or makes a face. No raves or tantrums.

Dressing   When I pick out his clothes for him and help him get dressed, he expresses his likes and dislikes for my selections in only a mild way. Never loudly disagrees with my selections, as his sister does.

Bath   Plays quietly in the tub with little talking or expression of feeling.

Play   Mostly likes to play quietly by himself, building with blocks or drawing.

People   His reactions to people, both new and familiar, tend to be low-key and fairly mild. Just a smile instead of shrieks of joy; just a frown instead of any dramatic expressions of dislike. Teddy does not like when his brother teases him, but he just walks away from the teasing.

Discipline   When praised or criticized, he reacts with a smile or frown, without any big explosions.

Expressions of feelings   Disappointment, pleasure, and enthusiasm all tend to be expressed mildly, through facial expressions rather than raising of his voice. When he cannot do something that he really wants to do, Teddy is likely to wander off or complain only briefly.

Pain   When hurt, he cries some, as one would expect of a four-and-a-half-year-old, but not as loudly or for as long as other children I know.

Intensity rating   Teddy is generally mild in his reactions and pretty laid back.

MOOD

Meeting new people   Along with withdrawing—being shy and inhibited—he usually wears a somber expression on his face. Sometimes a scowl or a look of discomfort.

Meeting familiar people   Somewhat glum at first, but he warms up after a little while and chats away with people he likes.

When waking   Not his best time! He is fairly consistently grumpy when he wakes up in the morning or from a nap.

When going to sleep   Usually he is fairly happy and pleasant before bedtime, unless he is unusually tired. Then he can be a little ornery.

When hungry   A bit grouchy when hungry, but no worse than most children his age.

During and after eating   Brightens up and becomes quite pleasant when he gets some food in his stomach.

(continued)

During bath, face and hand washing, and hair brushing   Used to fuss about these routines, but now he tolerates them fairly well. Usually less happy about nail cutting, though.

During dressing   Variable. Some days he actually enjoys it; other days he just tolerates it. Sometimes complains about having to make the effort.

While playing by himself   Teddy can happily play alone for a long time (often an hour or longer), singing, smiling to himself, and talking with his toy figures in imaginative play.

While playing with other children   He plays happily once he has gotten used to a child, and they have fun together.

When sick or injured   Not a big complainer. Sometimes it is hard to tell exactly how much he is hurting because of his mild and relatively soft, brief complaints.

Mood rating   Teddy seems about average in mood; shows a mixture of positive, cheerful and negative, gloomy responses.

PERSISTENCE AND ATTENTION SPAN

Play   Teddy plays with blocks or puzzles for long stretches, up to an hour at a time. If interrupted by a trip to the toilet or some other distraction, he usually returns quickly to the activity. It is hard to get him to stop when I need to go out on errands or to carpool the other children. When he receives a new toy, gets used to its novelty, and develops a liking for it, he will play with it for hours on end.

Tasks   For a boy his age, Teddy does pretty well at carrying out his few chores, such as putting his dirty clothes in the hamper. When I ask him to pick up the toys and clothes he has left scattered around his room, he can be counted on to stick to it for the five or ten minutes that it takes. When he and his big brother are supposed to do a chore together, it rarely goes smoothly, because they argue over who is doing the most work. But they get it done.

New physical skills   Teddy really works at these. Riding the tricycle was easy for him; he started when he was two and a half. Now he is working hard at mastering a two-wheeler. He is young for this, but he is determined and keeps asking for help from us. He ignores anyone who tries to distract him while he is working on this.

Listening to parents   Except when his hearing is off, thanks to ear infections, he pays attention to us when we tell him what we expect him to do. He does not always do as we ask, but there is no doubt that he listens and understands. His grandmother says this is because he is smart, but I think it is due to his ability to pay attention.

Looking at books   Just as he does with toys, Teddy spends long stretches looking at books that we have read to him. He tells the story to himself as he remembers it, or makes up imaginative, often funny revisions of the tale to vaguely match the pictures on the page.

Watching TV   Like most children, he likes to watch TV, and would keep his eyes glued to it if we didn't limit the children's TV time. But I have noticed that even when we are watching a program that he cannot fully comprehend, such as a newscast, he keeps listening and watching for longer periods than other children. It seems as if he is trying to grasp things beyond his reach. Sometimes he is so intent on watching that he squirms with the discomfort of needing to go to the toilet, so I have to remind him to take a quick break.

Persistence and attention span rating   Teddy rates quite high in this area.

DISTRACTIBILITY

During play and other activities   Teddy is hard to distract. He ignores, or seems to ignore, voices, music, the telephone, and other sounds around him while he is playing. The same with changes in lighting or people walking around him. Unlike his older brother, he generally sticks with his chores despite distractions. When I want to get his attention, I have to move right up next to him and touch him.

Pain   When he is hurt, has a bad earache, or has a sore throat, I usually find it hard to soothe him by holding him or by various tricks that tend to work with most children. Eventually he stops complaining.

Discipline   It is tough to redirect Teddy when he sets out to do something. Last night he started to bring all his blocks into our

(continued)

bedroom to build a space station, and I found it very hard to persuade him to stop and do it in his own room.

Distractibility rating   Teddy is low in distractibility.

SENSITIVITY

Sights   He seems quite aware of and responsive to changes in the appearance of things and people. Example: He commented about my new haircut on Saturday. (He said it was too short!)

Hearing   Teddy is usually the first in the family to hear a fire or police siren, or point out an airplane passing overhead. He is the first to be aware that the mail carrier is coming up the sidewalk. He has trouble falling asleep if there are loud or unusual noises in the house or outside in the neighborhood.

Touch   Quite sensitive. We hear frequent complaints about annoyances such as the scratchiness of a label inside his collar or the tightness of his socks or winter hats. The sheets on his bed have to be perfectly smooth—I switched to all-cotton from a polyester–cotton blend that pilled slightly after several washings. I barely noticed this, but Teddy did.

Smell   There is a little inconsistency here. Teddy is the first to notice when his baby sister has soiled her diaper. But on the rare occasions when he has had an accident in his pants or wet his bed, he claims that there is no odor at all.

Taste   When there is a minor variation in the way I prepare his sandwiches or when I put a different kind of jam on his toast, he always notices the difference and mentions it.

Social sensitivity   It is difficult to judge this in a four-and-a-half-year-old, but there are a few indications that Teddy is aware of other people's feelings. For instance, when his sister was younger and cried quite a lot, he used to be bothered by this and often began to cry soon after she started. Now, whenever his father makes a frown of disapproval—the children call it "Daddy's spilled milk face"—or when he smiles in praise of something, Teddy seems very tuned in to those expressions and visibly responds to them with a similar facial expression of his own.

Sensitivity rating   Quite sensitive.

CHAPTER TWO

How Your Child's Temperament Affects You

For most of the twentieth century, professionals who have studied child development have concluded that parents determine every aspect of children's behavior. If parents set clear standards and are consistent with discipline, yet loving and supportive, children generally turn out just fine. If parents are permissive, inconsistent, or unloving, their children are more likely to develop problems. Or so goes this line of reasoning.

A new body of research now questions the notion that parents are the single dominant factor in shaping behavior. This research suggests that the strongest effect on behavior is the interaction between parents and children. In other words, this is not a solo performance with the parent in the leading role, but a collaborative play whose costars—parent and child—share equal billing. Both parent and child contribute in this interaction, and both are affected by it.

These are confusing times for parents. Conflicting theories of child development still make it difficult to know what is most important for children. In the last twenty years yet another factor, a possible brain dysfunction, has been added as an influence on the interaction.

The child's temperament can enrich and support parent–child interaction, can disrupt it, or can have mixed results. In this interactive process, parents' feelings about, and reactions to, a child's temperament are as important as the temperament itself. How parents feel about temperament helps to determine how well or how poorly they accept or tolerate their child's temperament and how effectively they manage it.

Before discussing management techniques, it is essential first to understand how a child's temperament affects parents both as individual adults and as parents in their caregiving roles. Let's consider how one child's temperament affected her parents.

Lisa and Jack had postponed having children until they had established their careers and could afford to buy a home of their own. By their mid-thirties, they were ready. Their first child, Ben, had lived up to their expectations of the model baby, and they soon decided to round out their family with a sibling for him. During Lisa's second pregnancy, they redecorated the nursery, bought a new car seat, and fantasized about a full, happy life with their family completed. After a moderate labor and uneventful delivery, Tina arrived, beautiful at seven pounds, nine ounces.

Tina seemed particularly fretful to her parents during the first week at home. They took turns rocking her, pacing around the nursery, winding up musical mobiles, giving her more milk, changing her diaper, anything to try to get her back to sleep. Tina would eventually fall asleep only to awake within an hour or two. Her feeding schedule became no schedule at all, and Lisa nursed her whenever she cried.

After a few weeks, both Lisa and Jack were exhausted. Lisa believed that her breast milk must be insufficient, so she began formula supplements and eventually stopped nursing. This did not help. Tina's irregular feeding and waking patterns continued.

At first, Jack tried to help by getting up with Tina at night and taking on more of Ben's care; however, Jack had to rise at six o'clock each morning for work. In the evenings, he came home to a wife who was frazzled. Jack gradually withdrew from his share of caring for both children. He began to stay at work later to avoid arguments with Lisa over how to handle the baby. Most nights Jack slept downstairs on the sofa so he would not be awakened by Tina's cries. After two more weeks, both Jack and Lisa recognized what a strain the new baby was putting on their marriage. They often snapped at each other and rarely had any time or energy for intimacy. Although she had been successful with their first baby, Lisa began to feel inadequate as a mother, a wife, and a person. She wondered if she had made the wrong decision to have another baby. "Maybe I was not cut out for this mother role," she told herself, and then felt profoundly guilty about entertaining such thoughts. Jack felt badly as well, but he threw up his hands in frustration, turned away from his wife, and felt defeated. Each parent wondered, but did not tell the other, if their marriage could withstand this stress.

IMPACT ON PARENTS AS PERSONS

Before we look at how children's temperaments affect parents as caregivers, let's first consider the influence of temperament on parents as people. We have just seen how it can affect marital satisfaction in Jack and Lisa's situation. A child's temperament can have positive and negative impacts on parents' personal relationships, work performance, self-assurance, and various aspects of mental and bodily functions such as eating and sleeping.

Temperament also influences parents' overall sense of contentment or dissatisfaction and even their coping abilities. When a child's temperament frustrates them, parents may experience anger, guilt, anxiety, or depression, not only when they are with the child, but also throughout daily life. They may carry this worry with them into the workplace, with it in the back of their minds throughout the day.

Susan found herself staring at the computer screen at the insurance company where she worked. Instead of seeing columns of numbers, she envisioned the battle she had waged that morning with her five-year-old son about getting dressed and ready for school on time.

"It seems as if he's getting more poky and stubborn every morning," she thought. "He ignores me, almost as if he wants to upset me, when he knows I'm in a hurry to get to work."

Susan lost focus on her work as she replayed this scene in her mind's eye throughout the day. She even found that she was becoming snappish with coworkers for no apparent reason, until she realized that problems with her son were upsetting her so much that it affected her work.

When children's temperament traits annoy or frustrate parents, they may feel inadequate and deflated. Some parents may return to work sooner than they had planned or work longer hours because they believe that a teacher, day care worker, or babysitter can handle a child with bothersome temperament characteristics better than they can themselves. Some parents may go back to work quickly simply because child care is unpleasant for them. On the other hand, a mother may stay at home longer with a fussy infant because she feels that he needs more attention from her or that others would not understand or put up with him.

Temperament can also affect parents' social pride among their friends and community. Positive temperament traits can be a source of satisfaction: A child with high levels of activity and persistence, for instance, may excel at athletics, dance, or theater arts, which makes for proud parents. Other parents may feel embarrassed by some traits, such as shyness. For example, when Charlie withdraws and refuses to participate in events such as a neighborhood picnic, his parents feel embarrassed and assume that their friends think they have not adequately socialized him or are perhaps even being abusive toward him.

Temperament, and how parents feel about those traits in their own child, can even have an impact on parents' thought processes. If they are particularly upset by certain temperament traits, they may entertain irrational thoughts. An intense child, whose nearly every reaction is expressed in a loud voice and high pitch, led his mother to imagine that his intensity must have been caused by her worrying or something she ate during her pregnancy. Although it was unrealistic, she blamed herself for something she did not understand and had not learned to manage.

Temperament also influences a parent's coping style in the face of adversity. It can affect whether they confront problems head-on or avoid them. If their child's temperament drives parents up the wall, their sense of control can be shattered. A parent such as Susan, who successfully supervises several adults in the workplace, can become undone by a five-year-old whose intensity is consistently high, adaptability is low, and mood is negative. Susan finds herself overwhelmed with feelings of inadequacy as a person.

"I am a mature adult at work all day long. How can this child reduce me to a whining, screaming hyena at home?" she asks herself in frustration.

IMPACT ON PARENTS AS CARE-GIVERS

To understand the influence of temperament on parents as caregivers, let's begin by taking a look at the basic responsibilities of being a parent. Every parent has three essential tasks to ensure a child's well-being:

To provide food, protection, housing, and healthcare to supply the child's physical needs.

To offer stimulation, guidance, and affection to meet the child's developmental, behavioral, and emotional needs.

To teach family and community relationships to fulfill the child's socialization needs.

In the remainder of this chapter, we examine these parental tasks and see how a child's temperament may affect each area. There are, of course, several other major factors influencing how you function as a parent: your own experience as a child, your previous background and experience in providing child care, your pregnancy and early beginnings with your child, your health, your current stresses and supports, and other aspects of your child's personality. Here we discuss only temperament and the ways it can modify the care that parents give.

PHYSICAL NEEDS

Feeding

Nothing brings a parent and child into closer interaction than the act of feeding does. Although this is obvious with babies, even as children reach adolescence food is a central focus of much family interaction: what to eat, when to eat, how much to eat, where to eat. For example, Mom says "Finish your breakfast before you run for the bus," but the 16-year-old is already out the door with only a gulp of orange juice in her stomach and a piece of dry toast in her hand.

From birth, an infant is completely dependent on the parent to supply the right kind and amount of nourishment at appropriate times for normal sustenance and growth to occur. A new parent often wonders how much food is enough. The parent must also be able to read the baby's signals of hunger and satiety correctly. Many babies make their wishes known quite well; they cry with enough intensity and good timing to let their parents know they are hungry. They stop sucking or push the bottle or spoon away when they are full. They burp. They smile. Their clear messages help their parents give them what they need. Such reactions continue to influence parents' feeding practices throughout childhood.

If temperament confuses a parent about how hungry or full the baby may be, however, the parent may overfeed or underfeed the infant. Both can have physical consequences. This does not mean that parents knowingly overfeed or withhold nourishment from their children; they may offer more or less food as a result of the reactive style or temperament of the child.

Overfeeding can result from parents' attempts to quiet irritable infants by feeding them. They may believe that their infant is still hungry. Pleasant, agreeable children may also be overfed because they obligingly accept excessive food pushed on them by their parents. Some parents may fall into a routine of letting a fussy toddler carry a bottle around with her all day, and they automatically put a bottle of juice or milk in bed with her each night. These practices can lead to excessive weight gain or bottle-mouth dental cavities, a major decay of the upper-central teeth.

Underfeeding may occur with irritable children because their parents derive less gratification from the time-consuming activity of trying to feed children who spit out food, whine, squirm, and generally seem indifferent to whether or not they are fed. Other infants whose temperaments involve high adaptability, positive mood, low intensity, and low sensitivity—and who are therefore less prone to complaining about hunger—may also be underfed. These infants, whose temperaments make them uncomplaining, may not capture the attention of a busy or preoccupied parent who is not attuned to their less intense hunger signals.

In other words, a child must be able to grab the parent's attention to spark sufficient interaction and feeding. The parent's radar must pick up cues from the child, and the parent must get enough gratification from the feeding procedure itself for the child to be appropriately nourished. Feeding problems will be discussed in more detail in Chapter Six.

Temperament traits affect the parent–child feeding interaction in other ways as well. Easily distractible children interrupt the meal if sights or sounds capture their attention. A stream of sunlight that is making dancing patterns on the wall is just too fascinating for the baby to ignore, and so he turns away from the breast to watch. His mother may interpret this as a sign that he is full, even though he is still hungry. She buttons her shirt, puts him on her shoulder, pats his back, and puts him down for a nap. Three minutes later he is crying, and Mom does not know why.

A youngster whose physical activity level is high presents a great challenge for a parent who is trying to maneuver spoonfuls of pureed carrots into his mouth as he bounces and wiggles in his high chair. His father eventually loses patience and speaks sharply, and the baby has a tantrum. After several episodes of cleaning up carrot spray and other culinary messes, Dad loses interest in feeding his son and offers to do so less frequently.

A temperamentally irregular baby usually expresses hunger in an unpredictable fashion, which baffles and annoys most parents. Children with low initial approach and adaptability reveal these qualities even in the earliest months of life: They tend to be slow in attempting new foods and are resistant to new flavors or the consistency of various cereals. They do not readily accept a change in food temperature or in the timing or place of feedings, or even the person who is offering the food. Each of these traits has an impact on the parent's actions and feelings during feeding time.

PROTECTION

Helpless human babies have generated whole industries to protect them: intercom systems; car seats and railings; gadgets that child-proof doors and drawers; crib slats that must be close together so a head, an arm, or a leg will not become stuck; and so on. Ultimately, however, the parent is the child's primary protector. The parent is responsible for providing a safe environment, one free of toxins, pests, and other perils ranging from falling off beds to being physically, sexually, or psychologically abused. Whether a parent leans toward underprotection or overprotection depends largely on the interaction between parent and child, which in turn depends in part on how the child's temperament affects the parent.

Childhood accidents used to be blamed either on parents' inattentiveness or on the child's "accident proneness." Those who investigate accidents and teach risk prevention now conclude that diverse, interacting factors in the child, caregiver, and environment may all contribute to accidents. A look at these factors makes it apparent that highly active children—for example, infants who roll off the bed in a nanosecond when Mother's back is turned—present greater challenges to protecting them from accidents and injuries than do less active infants. Protecting them from injury is difficult, but it must be done. The role that temperament traits play in accidents will be discussed further in Chapter Six.

Studies have found that physical abuse of children results from a combination of factors in child, parent, and situation. Children who are physically abused may have temperament traits that include high intensity, negative mood, and other characteristics that, when combined, tend to make the child provocative or difficult to manage. Fussy babies and children who cry loudly and who are not easily pacified may be overdisciplined and even harmed, especially by parents who are experiencing a crisis such as loss of job or home, marital strife, or physical exhaustion. In these stressful situations, the child's temperament may be the spark that ignites parents' anger and pushes them over the edge. Feeling anger is normal; failing to restrain it is not.

Fortunately, most parents are able to control an impulse to strike or otherwise hurt a child when upset. Certainly not all children with difficult temperament traits bring their parents to contemplate physical violence; however, many do provoke their parents to verbal abuse and spanking. In all cases, abuse of a child is the parent's fault and is unacceptable. It cannot be excused because of the child's provocative behavior.

Other parents go to the other extreme in overprotecting children because they worry about potential disasters or are overly anxious about health and safety. This is common among parents whose child has had a serious illness early in life. The child's temperament comes into play as well. Irritability may add to the parent's concern about the child's health and well-being. If the child's temperament includes high physical activity, the parent may overprotect him by setting inappropriate, unnecessary limits when he attempts active games and sports.

The effects on health care provided by parents will be taken up in Chapter Six.

DEVELOPMENTAL, BEHAVIORAL, AND EMOTIONAL NEEDS

Most conscientious, well-informed parents recognize the importance of offering children stimulation, guidance, and affection. However, many parents with the best intentions do not understand how temperament differences in their children affect the meeting of these needs. In subsequent chapters we go into detail about the specific application of this information in various situations. For now, it is important to underscore one basic fact: A child's inborn temperament affects how and to what extent parents handle these basic behavioral and developmental requirements.

STIMULATION

In our current culture, parents are bombarded with advertisements and advice to "stimulate" their children from a very young age so that they will earn outstanding grades, gain acceptance to the right college, and be guaranteed a successful career. However, parents who best serve their children are not those who push their children with loads of stimulating toys, games, and experiences. Parents who best serve their children are those who understand and support their child's current level of functioning and are eager and able to help him build on present achievements to move to the next level. The question is, how do parents know what kind of child needs how much stimulation?

When it comes to temperament, the child who seems to benefit most readily from appropriate stimulation is one who is compliant and receptive to new things, is persistent at mastering new skills, and has a positive, pleasant mood. These temperament traits, in turn, reward the parent's efforts to provide a stimulating environment and encourage advancement to the next level. Another temperament trait that plays a key role in stimulation, at least in infants, is high activity. Active infants stimulate themselves into acquiring early motor skills by putting a lot of energy into practicing them.

A challenge for some parents is not to overstimulate or push children too fast or too soon. Many parents pressure their children in hopes of boosting their achievements and accelerating their development. How do different temperaments receive this overstimulation? A child who is very adaptable and has a positive, pleasant mood is more likely to tolerate parental pushing; a child who is less flexible is more likely to rebel against it.

Insufficient stimulation may be more likely to occur in circumstances in which the child's temperament fails to evoke enough positive caregiving from the parents.

GUIDANCE

In addition to appropriate doses of stimulation, parents also need to provide guidance, which some would call discipline, if their children are to achieve normal development and behavior. This guidance is provided by example, teaching, and approval of what is socially acceptable and disapproval of what is not. Chapter Three discusses specific ways to handle discipline with certain temperaments and situations. First, let's look at how temperament in general affects parent-child interaction in the area of guidance.

The way a child reacts—her temperament or style of behavior—has a profound effect on parents and on the effectiveness of their efforts to guide or discipline the child. A child who easily accepts and adapts to new things will comply fairly smoothly with the parents' efforts to guide her development and behavior. Take toilet training, for example. A pleasant, flexible child is more willing to sit on a potty chair, try it out, and return to it routinely than is a child who accepts novelty less readily, adapts to change slowly, and is persistent in refusing to use it.

How do these temperamental differences affect the parent as caregiver? The more compliant toddler is more likely to put parents at ease, make them think that this toilet training drama may not be as difficult as they had expected, and boost confidence in their own parenting skills. The child with the more resistant temperament may frustrate the calmest parents, leaving them stressed and feeling incompetent at this very basic child-rearing task. If the child is adamant in his refusal and the parents' stress continues to rise, they may overuse their authority or strength to force the child to sit on the potty or may engage in unnecessary criticism or abusive language. As mentioned earlier, irritable, unadaptable children can severely test the patience of even the best parents.

Some parents guide with tight reins, whereas others are at the opposite end of the guidance spectrum, setting insufficient limits. A high-spirited child whose temperament is intense, persistent, and stubborn about adapting to new rules or procedures can wear down parents. They may weaken or abandon the necessary limits they are trying to set because they feel tired or frustrated. It is simply easier at that moment to cave in to the child's demands than to maintain a steady strategy. A pattern of overindulgence is likely to develop, and the "spoiled" child will come to dominate the parents.

AFFECTION

Most parents try to love their children without qualification. They offer their acceptance, reassurance, and positive emotional support to their children. But as in all human relationships, the parent–child relationship is a mutual one, an interactive give-and-take. The quality of this relationship depends in considerable part on the child's temperament. How a child responds to expressions of love, affection, and caregiving on the part of his parents can encourage or discourage their next move in this interactive dance.

If we are honest, we will admit that some children are easier to love than others. It is easier to express affection to some more than to others because of their different temperaments. A child whose mood is generally friendly and upbeat, who pays attention when you are explaining something, who has a fairly regular rhythm to his daily routines, and who rarely complains, is so pleasant to have around that his parents reward him with lots of smiles, hugs, and other expressions of love and support. Each side of this relationship feeds the other with affection, and the relationship flourishes.

A child whose temperament causes more turbulence—for example, one who is stubborn about adapting to changes in routine, who frowns, sulks, and protests when asked to do a chore, or whose intensity tends to be high and abrasive—does not invite as much positive, warm interaction. His more trying temperament dampens his parents' overtures because they feel he does not reciprocate. They may unconsciously slide into a pattern of showing less affection, or they may even become hostile toward the child. Without intending to, these parents may demonstrate inadequate attention and affection, which can impair the child's self-esteem, motivation, and ability to develop close relationships with other people.

SOCIALIZATION

Children form their earliest important relationships within the family, the basic unit of social organization. Through interaction with parents, a child should discover a balance in relationships that is neither too distant nor too involved. Several aspects of temperament that have social components (such as approach to new people, mood, and adaptability) affect how children learn to live with other people within the family structure. This early experience helps to frame their expectations when forming adult relationships later in life.

A child's response to a new baby in the family offers a prime example of the role that temperament can play in early socialization experiences.

> *Jesse was three years old when his sister, Tonya, was born. Even before the baby arrived, Jesse's temperament was somewhat challenging for his parents to manage. He was slow to adapt, intense in his reactions, and highly sensitive to surrounding sights and sounds. Whenever Tonya cried because she was hungry, Jesse responded with yelling of his own.*
>
> *He usually complained whenever he was tired, and this response seemed to intensify with the arrival of the baby. As a rather active child, Jesse found it difficult to sit and play quietly when his mother told him that she had to nurse the baby. Instead, he insisted on climbing into the chair with her and the baby, dragging some toys with him, and wiggling around as his mother tried to nurse Tonya.*
>
> *As Jesse's mother came to understand his normal temperament, she was able to tolerate and accommodate it better. At the same time, she helped socialize Jesse by teaching him that his little sister was here to stay, a permanent part of the family. She made it clear to him that he was not allowed to disrupt Tonya's feeding but then she paid special attention to Jesse while Tonya napped.*

Socialization of the child for community relationships, for example, with neighbors, peers, teachers, is similarly affected by the sociability aspects of the child's temperament.

IMPACT OF THE CHILD'S TEMPERAMENT ON OTHERS

In addition to considering how your child's temperament affects you as parents, think about and make notes about the kind of impact it has on other important people in the child's life, that is, on siblings, grandparents, neighbors, friends, and teachers. Do they react the same way as you do, or are there significant differences?

PROBLEMS IN ADJUSTMENT

Your child may have some behaviors that concern you but that do not fit into the nine categories of temperament. If they are problems such as aggressiveness, noncompliance, underachievement, poor self-esteem, or impulsivity, they are likely to be adjustment problems. They should be listed on a separate page in your notebook and held until Chapter Four.

SELF-EVALUATION

Now that you have read about the nine temperament characteristics in Chapter One and observed them in your child, it is time to return to your notes and determine how these traits affect you. Which traits satisfy you, bother you, cause difficulty between you and your child, or cause friction within the family? Alongside your written observations from Chapter One, why not make a column for recording which traits you do and do not like? Or you may want to start a separate section in your notebook for this evaluation. There is no single formula for this exercise; whatever works for you is best.

As you consider how these various temperament characteristics make you feel, you may also find that you would like to continue your note taking about your child's temperament in ongoing situations. The more observations you make, the clearer some behavioral patterns may become.

In reviewing your observations of each temperament trait in your child, begin by asking yourself some questions: "Do I like this, or does it bother me? How much? Under which circumstances: at home, with relatives, in public? How does this make me feel?" Here are some examples about how several parents feel about different traits in their children.

> When he clings to my coat and won't say "hello" as I introduce him to new neighbors, I feel extremely embarrassed and wonder what they will think of me.

> When the baby fusses and squirms every time I try to dress her when I am in a hurry, I get really angry.

> When he laughs and splashes during bath time, I really enjoy it, no matter how soaked I get.

> When he adamantly refuses to wear his jacket on a 35-degree day, I am confronted with the impossible choice of a battle or giving in and feeling guilty.

> When he smiles and laughs on a day when I feel awful, I love him dearly.

> When she is moody and I can't find a way to cheer her up, I feel discouraged and helpless.

> When he daydreams, dawdles over his homework, but then draws a lovely picture for me, I feel conflicted.

> When she is so absorbed in practicing basketball that she won't come in for dinner, even after I have called her four times, I get very exasperated.

> When he warms up quickly to a new babysitter, I enjoy the rest of the evening without worrying about him.

> When people comment about some problematic aspect of my child's temperament or behavior, I feel like an inadequate parent.

> When she accepts changes in plans without a fuss, I feel good about her.

Your list will be much longer and tailored specifically to you and your child. The point of the previous examples is simply to suggest ways to begin looking at and measuring the impact that your child's temperament has on you. Undoubtedly, there will be traits that thrill you, give you quiet satisfaction, and make you burst with pride. Others will frustrate, irritate, and anger you. Many more may leave you with ambiguous or ambivalent feelings. Be sure to gauge your reactions to each trait separately. Perhaps even doing this exercise will change your perspective.

After reviewing all nine traits and thinking about how they affect you, ask yourself this broad, composite question: How does my child make me feel in general? This is not a simple question. If you are happy with your child overall, you are indeed fortunate. If you have a general sense of stress and conflict, then try to describe more precisely the emotional impact this has on you. What do those feelings do to you? What impact do they have on you and your functioning as a person and as a parent?

Think about the source of these feelings. Do they come just from the interactions with your child's temperament? If so, would other parents also find these particular temperament traits unappealing or difficult to tolerate? Traits such as negative mood or inflexibility, for example, do not win blue ribbons with most parents.

Does your difficulty with certain temperament traits also stem from not knowing how to manage these characteristics effectively? Do you feel that some of these traits might be welcomed and appreciated by other parents, but they are not qualities that you value or expected in your own children? Or is it the reverse?

A child with a high level of activity, for example, may delight athletic, outdoor-loving parents. But a whirling dervish of a toddler may confound parents who lead a quiet, sedentary life in a cramped apartment. Or a baby's fussiness might not bother you as much as it would other parents who are more sensitive to noises.

If certain qualities about your child upset you, also try to determine whether your feelings come partly or totally from sources other than the child. Consider whether your feelings stem from problems in your living situation, past or present. Do these feelings recall unpleasant ones from your own childhood? Could some of your concerns be related to financial, job-related, or marital stresses? Other children or relatives? Illness? Housing or neighborhood problems?

If other sources of stress are causing your discomfort, perhaps something about your child's behavior sets the match to the kindling. In other words, the problem or concern may not really originate with the child. Something about his temperament may strike an underlying nerve that has a root cause apart from the child.

PRIORITIZING

After you have determined which temperament characteristics satisfy you and which ones bother you, it is time to prioritize. Again, taking notes is helpful. Rank these traits according to those that bother you most, those you can tolerate, and those you can ignore. By prioritizing the areas that cause most concern, you will be ready to focus on particular suggestions in Chapter Three that can help you manage those traits so that your child can enjoy a better fit between temperament and environment.

Also list the traits that most please you. This can shed light on some positive traits that may have been taken for granted or underappreciated, characteristics that should be reinforced and supported as your child grows. It is very common for parents to focus primarily on negative behaviors and traits because they cry out for attention. But it is also important to notice the subtler, pleasant, satisfying aspects of a child's temperament. If you tell your child that her smile makes you feel good on this rainy day, or that he really can stick with a tough task, or that she is so observant when she mentions a bird chirping outside the window, you are rewarding the child with your attention and affection.

Before moving on to the next chapter, another point should be made. In considering how your child's temperament affects you, keep in mind that some of the traits that disturb you today may turn out to be plusses for your child in later years. Some traits become more tolerable or less strong as the child grows older, whereas others may become more challenging. Some traits are more acceptable in certain children than others, depending on age and gender. "Difficult" traits are likely to become less intense with time, and you may become more understanding and tolerant with experience.

High activity, for example, may bother parents of a toddler who has just started to walk because she is suddenly all over the place and into everything. As she gets older, although she still is a very active child, this trait can be channeled successfully into activities such as athletics or dance.

Distractibility is another temperament characteristic whose acceptance by parents may change over time. Distractibility can be a very desirable quality in an infant. Rattles, mobiles, music boxes, and lullabies help to distract him when he is fretful. Distractibility is not so welcome when he is in grade school, however, where the slightest interruption can steal his concentration away from his schoolwork and make learning more difficult.

Gender also affects how parents feel about certain temperament qualities. Shyness has been found to be tolerated more in girls than it is in boys. High activity is often better accepted in boys than it is in girls. This is not to say that girls should be shy and boys should not, or that boys should be more physically active than girls; it is simply the predominant way in which our culture tends to regard these traits in each gender.

Some parents may accept or value high activity in sons more than daughters because boys traditionally have had more outlets to express this trait, largely through sports and the generally accepted notion that "boys will be boys." But parents should also keep in mind that daughters with lots of physical energy can be encouraged, even from a very early age, to put this temperament trait to good use in areas such as dancing, gymnastics, soccer, basketball, softball, and other sports. Not only will this point her high activity in positive, productive directions, but the results can help to enhance her confidence and self-esteem.

Certain traits that concern parents at the present time can have benefits for the child now and later in life. Although some parents may wish that their shy child would be more socially outgoing, her slow approach to novelty can protect her in risky situations. She would probably be more likely to avoid dangerous strangers, for instance, than a child who is much more accepting.

Some traits that are seen as positive can actually have possible negative consequences. High adaptability is generally considered an advantage. A child who adapts quickly and smoothly to new situations tends to enjoy greater harmony with parents and other caregivers. This is a plus when the novel experience is a positive one, such as trying a new sport, going to camp for the first time, and starting a new school. Yet highly adaptable children may also accept negative influences too readily. They may be more easily persuaded by peers and others to experiment with risky behaviors when they approach adolescence, that is, smoking, drinking, experimenting with drugs, and having unprotected sex.

As you consider your child's temperament traits and how they affect you at this moment, keep in mind that these traits, while they remain fairly stable through life, will have different influences and outcomes at different ages. If your child is easily distracted in second grade, for example, do not assume that he is doomed for life. Take heart from the example of one of the most productive geniuses in history, Leonardo da Vinci, who has been described by historians as frequently distracted by minutiae, who rarely completed anything he began, and who wrote disjointed collections of notes for books that he never got around to writing. The distractible Leonardo was the ultimate Renaissance man: artist, inventor, astronomer, and engineer.

The following table suggests both challenging and welcome aspects of each of the nine temperament traits. You may want to go over this table as you review your observations of your child's temperament and consider how they affect you. Keep in mind that temperament traits are neither good nor bad. What matters is the fit.

HOW TEMPERAMENT AFFECTS CHILDREN AND THEIR PARENTS

This table illustrates how each of the nine temperament traits can have beneficial, gratifying aspects as well as challenging, unpleasant dimensions.

TRAIT	SOMETIMES NEGATIVE ASPECTS	GENERALLY POSITIVE ASPECTS
ACTIVITY	*High:* Social activities and task performance are easily interfered with. May be mislabeled "hyperactive." Hyperactivity is disorganized, purposeless activity and not simply high activity.	*High:* Vigorous and energetic; explores surroundings; stays active in dull environments.
	Low: Slow to perform tasks; may seem drowsy; may be labeled "lazy."	*Low:* Less disruptive in cramped environments and circumstances.
REGULARITY	*High:* May be a problem if the environment cannot provide for needs on schedule.	*High:* Few surprises for parents and other caregivers.

TRAIT	SOMETIMES NEGATIVE ASPECTS	GENERALLY POSITIVE ASPECTS
REGULARITY	*(continued)*	
	Low: Unpredictable care requirements.	*Low:* May not be bothered by irregularities in caregiving or routine events.
INITIAL REACTION	*Approaching or bold:* May accept negative influences too quickly, which is dangerous in hazardous environments.	*Approaching or bold:* Makes a rapid fit in favorable settings.
	Withdrawing or inhibited: Slow to accept change; may avoid useful experiences.	*Withdrawing or inhibited:* Cautious in dangerous situations, e.g., in accepting offers from strangers.
ADAPTABILITY	*High:* In danger of accepting negative influences, such as antisocial values of peers.	*High:* Generally at an advantage; accepts positive influences more quickly; in greater harmony with caregivers.
	Low: May have difficulty adjusting to requirements of caregiving; stress-producing; may be labeled "difficult."	*Low:* Less likely to accept negative influences.
INTENSITY	*High:* Abrasive and annoying; may evoke counterintensity; may mislead parents or other	*High:* Needs are certain to get attention; caregivers welcome the positive intensity.

TRAIT	SOMETIMES NEGATIVE ASPECTS	GENERALLY POSITIVE ASPECTS
	caregivers as to serious-ness of an issue or illness.	
	Low: Needs may not be expressed with enough forcefulness to be recognized.	*Low:* Easier to live with.
MOOD	*Positive:* May be too posi-tive and upbeat about real problems.	*Positive:* Generally welcome.
	Negative: Unpleasant for parents and other care-givers who may overesti-mate importance of an issue or physical complaint.	*Negative:* Few advan-tages; however, may evoke more positive involvement from par-ents and other caregivers because of their concern.
PERSISTENCE AND ATTENTION SPAN	*High:* Being absorbed in work and play may make the child seem to ignore parents, teachers, and others.	*High:* Greater achieve-ment likely at various tasks and school performance.
	Low: Less efficient at task performance; fails to per-form as expected. Not to be considered an "attention deficit" if the child func-tions well, particularly in combination with com-pensatory factors such as high adaptability and intelligence.	*Low:* May be more easily drawn out of activities or habits that are unacceptable to parents and other care-givers.

TRAIT	SOMETIMES NEGATIVE ASPECTS	GENERALLY POSITIVE ASPECTS
DISTRACTIBILITY	*High:* Easily diverted from tasks; performance is easily interfered with; needs reminders.	*High:* Easy to soothe as an infant.
	Low: May be unaware of important signals such as warnings from parents.	*Low:* Can work efficiently in noisy places.
SENSITIVITY	*High:* More perceptive of surrounding noises, smells, lights, textures, and internal sensations; as an infant, more prone to colic and sleep disturbances.	*High:* More aware of changes in environment and of existence and nuances of other people's thoughts and feelings.
	Low: May miss important cues from surroundings.	*Low:* More shielded from too much environmental input.

Adapted from William B. Carey and Sean C. McDevitt. Coping with Children's Temperament: A Guide for Professionals. *New York: Basic Books, 1995; Table 2.1, pp. 16–17.*

CHAPTER THREE

Managing Your Child's Temperament

After profiling your child's temperament and exploring its effects on you, you are now ready to consider various ways to manage your child's unique temperament more effectively. This chapter begins with a broad perspective before proceeding to focus on the nine individual temperament characteristics and how to handle the ranges within each of them. We ask you to resist the temptation to flip ahead to find the trait that bothers you most. First, please read the general information at the outset because it sets the stage for more specific management approaches later in this chapter.

THE GOAL: EFFECTIVE PARENTING

Although you cannot change your child's temperament, you can work with it to improve its fit with your parenting techniques. You can appreciate and support the positive traits that delight you and that promote your child's functioning, growth, and development. You cannot, however, hammer the undesirable traits out of a child through rigid discipline, bribery, attempts at reasonable persuasion, or other tried-and-failed methods. You can learn to accept those traits and—at the same time—develop alternative ways to manage your child's temperament to reach the immediate objective: reduced stress and increased harmony in parent–child interactions.

The larger goal is more effective parenting. Accomplishing this does not mean that you should always expect to be a perfect parent. Effective parenting is being able to read your child's behavior correctly and help her mature successfully by meeting her needs for stimulation, guidance, affection, and socialization. It also means striving to do this fairly consistently and modifying as needed.

THE FOUR R'S

Before we get specific, here is a general strategy to consider first. Try using the four R's: recognition, revision, relief, and referral.

RECOGNITION

Based on the information in Chapter One, you should now be able to recognize your child's unique patterns of reaction in various situations. Equally important is making the distinction between temperament, other behavioral issues apart from temperament, and a mixture of the two.

REVISION

With this recognition and the information about temperament in general comes a revised understanding of the behaviors that have been troublesome. You should have a better sense of which behaviors are temperamental characteristics that you did not consciously or unconsciously cause. A new perspective should emerge with greater respect for yourself and your child, with less guilt, anger, and fears about your parenting. Your confidence can be bolstered by knowing that temperament can be managed and that bothersome traits tend to lessen with good care and may even become assets. Much of the rest of this chapter discusses specific coping techniques for reducing the stress generated by those traits.

RELIEF

When a child's temperament is really wearing parents down and causing considerable stress in their marriage or in the family, parents need some relief. They need to recharge their energies through rest and relaxation. They need to get out of the house for an evening or a weekend. Yet many parents feel too overwhelmed or overworked to take time for themselves. They may feel embarrassed or ashamed to seek help, even if it is only to ask a friend to watch the children for an evening or a sister-in-law to take them for the weekend. If this is how you feel, try to overcome this hesitancy because a break from a tense routine can benefit everyone. Many parents are helped by putting their children in day care for a few hours a week. Support groups can also offer encouragement and information about managing children such as yours. (See the Resources section at the end of this book.)

REFERRAL

If your child's temperament is particularly difficult to handle, you may want to discuss this with a professional such as your child's physician or a mental health specialist. (More about this in Chapter Four.) Parents should be cautioned that many professionals know little about temperament, and they may offer incorrect diagnoses or plans of management. The temperament may be blamed on physical problems or even your own management. You can better make the decision whether to seek help after reading this chapter and Chapter Four and seeing how this information applies to your child.

In the descriptions of the nine traits that follow, you will find some specific suggestions about what you can do or say in various circumstances. Let's begin with some general principles:

- Avoid critical descriptions of your child in any situation. Calling a child who is not very active a "slowpoke" or "lazy bones" will not help to change or improve the situation, and it can make matters worse. Instead, offer suggestions and choices that deal with the troublesome reaction or behavior without demeaning the child with a label. Specific positive language suggestions are given later in this chapter as we discuss specific temperament traits.

- As your child moves into the toddler and preschool years, begin to talk about temperament traits with the child in an age-appropriate way that the child can comprehend. This will let your child know that you understand and acknowledge her temperament, and as she grows, it will also help her form a clearer and more positive self-image.

- Develop your own inventory of useful phrases for handling various stressful situations as you go along. These phrases should be tailored to your individual child and the situation. Use language that feels comfortable to you. Keep adding to this repertory and varying your words because children are very quick to detect repetitive phrases. When they start to roll their eyes, you will know that it is time to rewrite your script.

- Beware of being too democratic, offering lengthy explanations, and giving the child too much leeway and too many choices. Try to stay in control and be concise about acceptable alternatives to the current behavior that you want to redirect. Being authoritative and affectionate is better parenting than trying to be a friend to your child.

MANAGING TRAITS FOR EFFECTIVE PARENTING

In the following sections, management suggestions are offered for each of the nine temperament traits. These suggestions apply to both extremes of each trait: for example, high distractibility and low distractibility; negative and positive mood; the high end of regularity and the very low or unpredictable end of the spectrum; and so forth. Your child's temperament may be nearer one end than the other, or it may be somewhere in the middle. But *all* of these variations are normal. Take into consideration how you can best adapt these suggestions to your child's individual reaction patterns in the situation at hand.

ACTIVITY

High   As with other temperament characteristics, high activity is neither all bad nor all good. It is the fit that matters most. Many times, parents delight in their child's spirited, boundless energy. But in tight quarters or settings in which high levels of activity are inappropriate (as in a theater or crowded grocery aisle), physical activity requires some reining in or alternative outlets. For example, before leaving, you can instruct the child that he must sit quietly when in the theater; however, you also might suggest that he can go outside and run around for a while during intermission or after the show. As another example, you can give the child an opportunity to be very active before going grocery shopping, perhaps with a brief stop at a playground on the way; however, she needs to know that running in the store is not permitted.

Remember that highly active children are almost always completely normal and not brain injured or overstimulated. If you are concerned there might be a physical basis for your child's high activity level, check this out with the physician.

For children with highly active temperaments, it is useful to have plans and backup plans to deal with, but not necessarily curb, their energy. Have a supply of projects, tasks, and games that will help burn energy and channel it along constructive paths. For a baby who is crawling and starting to walk, a roomy but safe home environment is essential. Whenever possible, let her climb up and down stairs and roam from room to room, rather than confining her to a single room, crib, or playpen.

Older children need plenty of time and opportunity to climb jungle gyms, race around playgrounds, kick soccer balls, and participate frequently in many types of physical activity. If the home or school environment is not conducive to high activity, try to find other outlets.

The Engels lived in a small city apartment far from a park or playground. Their children attended a school with a tiny playyard in which students spent only fifteen minutes a day. Recognizing that their children had very active temperaments, the Engels decided to make an adventure out of going to school each morning. Instead of taking the bus, they arose fifteen minutes earlier and walked with their children to school. Along the way, they made a game of turning each block into a different physical activity: skipping, walking backward, taking huge strides, hopping, and jumping over cracks in the sidewalk.

The Engels also found an after-school program at a neighborhood recreation center at which the children participated in supervised activities: basketball, floor hockey, gymnastics, and swimming. These outlets made the children calmer at home and less "rammy," as Mrs. Engel described their previous frenetic activity.

Highly active children usually need some transition time to unwind, just as athletes need cool-down exercises at the end of strenuous physical activity. Children cannot reasonably be expected to switch off their high energy immediately and sit down to read a book or fall asleep. If they are racing about the house when you want them to calm down for a meal or at bedtime, it helps to guide them into a quieter activity first, such as gentle bouncing on a cushion or making a game of moving in slow motion. For an active infant, motion such as rocking, pacing, or stroking the back can help smooth the transition from activity to a more placid pace.

A word of caution: Children with high-activity temperaments may not display signs of fatigue as obviously as other children do because they always seem to be on the go, even when they feel tired. Their need for rest and sleep can easily be overlooked. Be sure that they get enough rest. These children need it as much, if not more, than less active youngsters.

When talking with highly active children, do not label them "hyper," "wild," or "bad." Instead, describe their activity favorably, such as "energetic," "vigorous," or "active," and suggest a more acceptable option when possible. The Engels use expressions such as these: "You are a fast runner, but the people here in the supermarket don't want kids racing around. Save your running for the playground later." "We know you like to jump off the beds, but the loud thumping upsets the neighbors downstairs." "You're a wonderfully energetic kid, but right now your speed is a bit too much for Grandma's kitchen. Why don't you go out and play in her yard until it is time to eat?"

Low Children who are low in activity simply move slowly and not very much, which does not mean that they have no ambition and will never complete activities, tasks, and games. They are not trying to test how far they can push their parents with their slow tempo.

These children need to be given enough time to complete tasks. What counts is that the job be done adequately and without prodding. This is much more important than performing it perfectly or in record time just to please their parents. When these children do complete the job, they deserve to be complimented on finishing it without mentioning how long it took them to do so.

It is not helpful to call these children "lazy" or "poky." Instead, try to acknowledge that although you understand their slower pace, certain things need to be done at certain times and within certain time limits. For example, you might try expressing it this way: "I know you like to take your time when you put your blocks back on the shelf, but we have to go shopping in ten minutes." Or "You like your quiet indoor games, don't you? But Johnny is waiting for us outside with his bike."

Some parents find that an effective, reasonable way to speed up young low-activity children without criticizing or condemning them is to give them a kitchen timer, an hourglass, or a digital clock. These props give young children a concrete way to conceptualize time. When they can see grains of sand sliding into the bottom of the hourglass or watch digital numbers change on the face of a clock, they can better grasp the time limits that you have set for them to finish whatever they are doing.

REGULARITY

High Children with this trait are quite predictable. They enjoy following a schedule because it feels right to them, not because they are afraid of variations. Parents do well to provide these children with a reasonably regular schedule in the early years. This can be challenging for many busy families, particularly parents whose workday does not always end at a precise time.

If parents' schedules are changed at the last minute, it can be upsetting for a child with a highly regular temperament. For these children, some advance warning is reassuring. If they expect to be picked up at an after-school program or a friend's house exactly at 6 P.M. and parents are delayed at work, Mom or Dad could phone and explain, "I'm sorry, I will be a little late, but I can't wait to see you. When we get home we can fix dinner together, because I know we'll both be as hungry as bears."

As children grow older, they become better at finding their own ways of accommodating life's irregularities. The more parents accept this trait in the early years and help their children expect occasional bumps in their well-ordered lives, the more these children will be able to handle unpredictable events with flexibility in later years.

Low Certain children seem to come unequipped with internal clocks. Their unpredictability is not caused by anything a parent did, nor is it deliberate on the child's part. It is simply the way the child functions.

During infancy, parents need to be very flexible in trying to meet a baby's eating and sleeping needs as they occur. However, even the most irregular infant can be coaxed gradually to conform with a more regular schedule even if the infant's tendency still is to be irregular. Some infants' schedules are more easily reorganized than others are, of course. If your infant is more unpredictable than you would like, do not become so discouraged that you give up trying. Instead, keep plugging away, as Tina's parents learned to do.

Recall how Lisa and Jack—in Chapter Two—were stressed by their newborn's irregularity and irritability. When they discussed this with Tina's pediatrician and learned more about temperament traits, they discovered that Tina's temperament, and not her mother's breast milk, lay at the heart of their problems. Lisa did not have to stop nursing.

At the pediatrician's suggestion, Tina's parents gradually reorganized her schedule. Whenever she slept longer than four hours during the day, they woke her up and fed her. If she awakened only two hours after being fed, they did not feed her immediately; instead, they held off and increased the number of minutes before feeding her again. They also learned soothing techniques other than feeding to calm her when she fussed: talking quietly to her, playing with her, rocking her, and giving her a pacifier.

From the toddler years on, parents can impose regular mealtimes and bedtimes; however it is important that they not insist the child be hungry or fall asleep exactly at an appointed hour. An irregular child should not be criticized for this trait. He simply is expected to join the family at the table for a meal, even if he is not hungry at that moment.

Monica's mother was successful in bringing a little more regularity to the life of her seven-year-old without criticizing Monica's natural tendency to become hungry at irregular times. Her mother often used statements such as this: "I know you are not hungry right now, but we would like you to come and sit with us at the table, talk with us, and try to eat something while the food is hot."

Although Monica continued to be hungry at odd times, this trait became less of a problem as she gradually began eating with the family at regular mealtimes. Most likely, she will still sometimes need naps or snacks at unexpected times.

School-age children can be held accountable for meeting certain basic deadlines, such as being ready for the school bus in the morning, getting home by a specified time, and completing homework by the teacher's assigned date. Low regularity can make these requirements difficult to meet; however, this temperament trait can be guided. For example, stickers or gold stars on the calendar can be awarded for days when the child arrives at the bus stop before the bus.

INITIAL REACTION

Approaching or bold   Entering unfamiliar territory is easy for children whose initial approach is outgoing. They are not fazed by new people, places, or situations. They shift gears comfortably when meeting new children on the playground, when entering a classroom for the first time, or when any social spotlight focuses on them.

This temperament is generally an asset because it promotes adjustment. A child's initial acceptance of novelty may not last. When the appeal wears off, the child's zest may wane. After a burst of enthusiasm for playing with the new children on the block, for example, Rashida decided that she really preferred her old friends.

This ready approach also can place a child at risk in certain situations. Because talking with strangers in an elevator, for example, may seem natural to outgoing children, parents need to teach them appropriate precautions in such situations. Without criticizing the child or the temperament, a parent might say "I like the way you are so friendly with people, but you should not tell strangers your name or where you live. And you should never go anywhere with somebody you do not know."

Withdrawing or inhibited   Many children are timid about new experiences. It is simply the way they are. This trait should not be confused with a dislike of the new experience, specific fear based on a previous traumatic event, or lack of cooperation. Nor should you assume that inhibition means that the child's initial rejection is her final answer.

> *When Mary's mother said "If you don't want to go to Sally's birthday party, okay, then, I won't take you," she misread Mary's initial, hesitant response. Mary was shy about going to a birthday party of a classmate whom she hardly knew. But, her initial reluctance did not mean she absolutely refused to go. With some time to think about it, Mary may well have decided to attend the party.*

Parents can help children with this temperament by preparing them for novelty and allowing them some reasonable time to adjust. Parents can explain plans and details ahead of time and practice or role-play reactions to such situations. Mary's mother might have said, for example, "I know you have never been to Sally's house before, and there will probably be a lot of new kids at her party. Maybe you would like to go for a little while and see what it's like. If you are having fun, you can stay. If you want to leave after a few minutes, you can come home."

> *It is also helpful to call attention to a shy child's previous successes. Mary's mother could have added, "I remember that you*

were not sure whether you wanted to go to Kareem's party last
year. But after you got there, you said you had a ton of fun."
For best results, Mary's mother would leave it at that.

When a child's initial response to novelty is withdrawing or inhibited, she should not be put on the spot or pushed too hard. If Mary's mother used the previous success of overcoming shyness to badger Mary into attending Sally's party, it probably would backfire. A parent can urge or encourage in a gentle way; however, shoving the child overboard to sink or swim can be counterproductive and even harmful.

If a withdrawing child is about to attend a new day-care center, school, or camp, it is useful to make an introductory visit so the child can see the place and begin to form an idea of what to expect. It is also important to praise your child immediately after a difficult experience: "That couldn't have been easy to try out for a new team when you didn't know the coach or other players. You were really brave."

Parents can also teach specific social skills for overcoming initial inhibition, such as how to shake hands and introduce oneself when meeting someone new, how to get started on play activities, how to answer the telephone politely, and how to speak clearly if the child tends to mumble.

A shy, withdrawing child should not be scolded, ridiculed, or shamed for this temperament trait. Telling a child, "Don't be so shy" is not helpful; it only makes the child more uncomfortable. Instead of criticizing, parents can support the child with encouraging statements such as these: "I know this is new for you, and new situations can be tough." "It's all right if you want to take some time to get used to this." "How about if you watch and think about it for a few minutes?" "I know you have never tried this new food and that it doesn't look much like other foods you enjoy, but maybe you'll be surprised by how good it tastes."

As your child grows up, you will undoubtedly notice that he appears less inhibited and withdrawing when faced with new people and unfamiliar settings. Yet, your child may still *feel* shy because his temperament is essentially the same. His more extroverted responses result from the experiences of learning how to change the way he reacts outwardly in order to get along better in the world.

ADAPTABILITY

High   Adaptable children readily accept changes that are expected of them. This flexible cooperation or openness is generally a welcome asset; however, it does not mean that these children will accept anything at all. When talking with children who have a high adaptability, praise them for their cooperation or flexibility and do not take their adaptability for granted: "Joe, I am really proud of the way you pitched in and helped take care of your little cousins while Aunt Maddy and I were getting dinner ready. I know they are not your favorite playmates."

Parents also need to be cautious if the highly adaptable child seems too willing to incorporate undesirable ideas, values, or behaviors witnessed among peers or on television. Parents should monitor their child's exposure to such negative influences.

Low   Life presents many changes that require us to adjust. Children with low adaptability have difficulty making adjustments to changes in their lives and accepting the ongoing requirements of their living situations. But parents should not assume that their resistance means they cannot change at all or are completely unwilling to do so. These children just need a little extra time, preparation, advance warning, and support to adjust.

Household rules and regular daily routines are essential for every family's well-being, and children must learn to accept them. Parents need to set limits and state their expectations clearly and firmly. They are in charge, and they need to let children know it. These statements certainly are not intended to revive authoritarian, Victorian-era discipline; however, parents can and should be *authoritative*.

Although is not always easy to be firm, consistent, and calm, parents can strive toward that goal because it provides structure and stability in the family and reassures the children. They may fight it, and you; however, children and adolescents want to know where they stand. They want to know what the rules are and what their parents expect of them. Parents who are simultaneously authoritative and affectionate send the clear message that they care about their children.

It is important to pay attention to this temperament trait because low adaptability can reduce children's chances of success in personal relations, achievements, and other opportunities. Parents, therefore, need to help children through the more difficult challenges. Some suggestions follow:

- The number of adaptations your child must make can sometimes be reduced or spread out over time. This takes thought and effort to plan ahead but helps lessen stress and friction for both the child and the adults involved. Why not avoid unnecessary changes?

- The adjustment can be broken down into stages or parts, such as inviting a new babysitter to meet and play with the child for an hour or so with a parent present. The child will then be more comfortable when the sitter returns two nights later and the parents go out for the evening.

- Warnings and explanations can be given about impending challenges, such as a shift in household rules, a change in mealtimes or bedtimes, a visit from relatives, or unexpected events, such as missing a favorite gymnastics class because it is the only time a dental appointment is available.

Michael's parents began planning a first-time family trip to the beach weeks ahead by showing their son library books about the seashore and shells. They bought him a plastic bucket and shovel for the backyard sandbox. They explained that they would be staying in a cottage during their vacation and that Michael would be sleeping in a new bed. They told him all about Aunt Jane, with whom they would be sharing the beach house.

By the time the vacation arrived, Michael was fairly well prepared; however, his parents still did not push him. For example, well before bedtime arrived, they suggested he take a look at his new bed, bounce on it, and lie on it. They brought along the same night-light he used at home. They did not urge him to go into the ocean. Mom and Dad knew their son well enough to accept the fact that he required a bit more time and opportunity to adapt than their other children do. When the vacation was over, Michael was having such a good time that he did not want to leave.

Social skills can be taught. Children with low adaptability feel more assured about making necessary adjustments if they have the proper tools. If a child resists going to grandparents' house for a big holiday meal, for instance, the parents can help the child feel more at ease by teaching him—by rehearsing or role-playing—manners and conventions that will be expected: how to respond to Uncle Rosco's jokes; how to decline the lime-green gelatin salad with a polite "No, thank you"; when to say "May I please be excused?" if they have finished eating; how to find quiet ways of amusing themselves while adults talk; how to survive Grandma's big wet kisses.

When a difficult adaptation is successfully achieved, the child should be praised. This is an effective way to encourage further flexibility in the future. Little is gained by accusing the child of being stubborn. Instead, understanding statements such as these are helpful: "I know it is not easy for you to make rapid changes, but you were really quick and cooperative when Grandma asked you to . . ." "I realize that you need more time for changes like this."

"I understand that you like to think things over before making decisions, but . . ." "I know that you want to know what to expect beforehand." "I am proud of the way you made yourself try out for a part in the class play. It must have been hard to get up on that stage."

INTENSITY

High It is easy to misread children's high intensity—their loud, high-energy responses—as genuinely strong feelings about whatever sets off the response. An emphatic no does not necessarily mean your child will never try the new food, never play with the classmate who has invited him to his house, or never wear those new sneakers that just put you in debt. While intense negative responses can be upsetting, intense positive ones can be joyful. What a difference between a screamed refusal and a loud declaration of affection, yet both are signs of intensity.

Children with high intensity seem to operate consistently at a turned-up volume. There is little dullness with these children; they are indeed dramatic. However, their intense responses can be an exaggeration or may be misread as bad manners.

Their dramatic responses to different events may appear to be of equal importance; in reality they probably are not. Parents need to learn to read the true meaning of these reactions. After a stumble on the playground, does the child's wailing reflect serious injury, or is it simply a reflection of his intense temperament? Is she really ill when she complains loudly about stomach pains, or is this her standard response to any discomfort?

A common mistake that parents make is responding to a child's intensity with an equally intense reply, such as screaming back at a child who has just yelled about something inconsequential. Another mistake is giving in to the child's loud demand simply to make peace.

A better response is to meet the child's intensity with composure in an even, firm, but understanding voice. State your recognition of the problem at hand. Rather than criticizing the child's volume or demanding tone, a parent can talk calmly about the real issue and not the way in which the child expressed it. This not only diminishes stress in the immediate situation but also helps the child understand and regulate her intensity by herself.

Statements such as these are suggested. "I know you have a good, strong voice, but I will come to you just as soon if you ask me for help in a softer, quieter voice." "Your enthusiasm is exciting, but now it's time to unwind and relax before bedtime."

Low   It is much easier for most parents to live with children who have low intensity. There are fewer surprises and explosions. Yet a child who responds with low intensity, that is, with little drama, a low voice, and little pep, may be viewed incorrectly as lacking enthusiasm or feeling. This can be entirely misleading. Mildly expressed feelings and thoughts may be as important to this child as those expressed loudly by noisier, more intense children.

Parents need to watch and listen carefully to pick up on the feelings of children with low intensity. With infants and toddlers, who have yet to acquire the verbal language necessary to express themselves, parents can judge the importance of the child's reaction by other clues, such as facial expression and body language. With an older child, parents can discuss the given situation with the child to determine the true strength of his feelings or convictions.

MOOD

Positive   Friendly, pleasant reactions are almost always welcome and rewarding for parents. We love these sunny children. However, parents must not assume that all is well all of the time. A child with a positive disposition may smile even when in considerable anguish.

It is important not to dampen the child's cheerful spirit. Approve of positive responses: "The doctor's receptionist mentioned how glad she was to see you again. She said you are one of their friendliest patients." "You really cheered up Uncle Fred when he wasn't feeling well." "Dan's mother told me that she always enjoys your visits because you're so pleasant to have around."

Parents must also teach and remind children when outgoing, friendly approaches are inappropriate and when certain situations may make their behavior dangerous, such as meeting a stranger when walking home from school.

Negative   An unpleasant, unfriendly style of responding to stress and change can be assumed to be a normal inborn tendency, unless there is evidence of an adjustment problem. An adjustment problem is a distinct emotional or behavioral disturbance, such as hostility or aggression (see Chapter Four). Some children simply do not come equipped with sunny dispositions. Although many do, parents of such children should not feel guilty or think that they have harmed their child.

> *Irene's first child had a pleasant disposition from the time she was an infant. When she was away at camp, she signed her letters home, "Happy as always, Jenny." Irene loved and appreciated this quality in Jenny but worried that she might have failed Tracy, her younger child, whose temperament was more somber.*
>
> *"I often wondered if there was something I failed to do with Tracy that I did do with Jenny." Irene was relieved to recognize, however, that she had not failed Tracy in any way. Her daughters simply had different temperaments when it came to mood.*

When children fuss, complain, or otherwise respond with a negative mood, it is difficult for parents not to become angry. However, anger and criticism do not help the child, or the situation. The unpleasantness may be an exaggeration of the child's real feelings. Try to determine those true needs without overrating or overdiagnosing them.

Ignore as much of the child's negativity as you think reasonable, keeping in mind that sometimes the cause of the complaining can be quite real to the child even though it may seem trivial to you.

Parents can help older children reduce their negative tendencies that get in the way of personal relationships. Insist on good manners, for instance. Suggest ways of responding that will make sense to the child, such as "Tyler might be more willing to play with you if you smile at him instead of scowling." Or "When you meet Tyler, how about saying something nice instead of ignoring him? I bet that would make him want to share his toys with you."

In talking with children whose moods lean toward the negative, try not to scold them for this trait. Express understanding and acceptance, while at the same time offering constructive suggestions: "I know that you tend to stay annoyed for a while, but it's time to move on." "These new social situations are likely to make you feel uncomfortable, but please try not to let your friend, or her mother, feel as if it's her fault."

PERSISTENCE AND ATTENTION SPAN

High   This trait can be a tremendous advantage for a student or an adult. In toddlers and young children, however, it can be an extraordinary challenge for parents and other caregivers: These children reach, poke, pull, and explore, diligently like agents targeted on a crucial mission. They do not want to stop their play activities. They seem unaware of a parent's call to come to the table or go to bed.

Refrain from calling your child "stubborn," although that may be what you are thinking. Instead, try to give advance warnings: "We need to leave in fifteen minutes, so I'll tell you in ten minutes that it will be time to put the toys away." You also can avoid battling with children who have this trait by preventing them from starting a new or lengthy activity if the time available is short. Such tactics can help you avoid or shorten some unnecessary tests of wills.

Parents can help children with high persistence recognize that it is difficult to leave something they enjoy when an adult says it must stop: "I know it's hard for you to stop building that terrific castle, so I want you to know now that supper will be ready in ten minutes. You can go back to the blocks after you have finished eating." Parents also should acknowledge successes: "Thanks for coming as soon as I called." Older children who persist at homework or household chores also deserve parental praise; for example, "I think it's great that you try so hard," and "I really appreciate your help in folding all those clothes from the dryer."

With some highly persistent children, it may be advisable to remind them that it is impossible for anyone to achieve perfection at everything. These children may need help turning off their highly persistent efforts from time to time. They need to be persuaded that prolonged effort on some tasks may not be necessary and may be taking too much attention and energy from other things, such as games and friendships.

Low   This temperament trait presents a mixed bag of advantages and disadvantages. In infants and toddlers, low persistence may be a relief to parents because it can mean fewer power struggles and prolonged, dangerous, or simply annoying explorations of the house or outdoors. Enjoy this trait while your child is very young. Low persistence has a downside in that in older children it means they are less likely to follow through on household tasks and schoolwork. They may need frequent reminders to put their things away, hang up their jackets, make their beds, take the dog for a walk, and complete their homework on time. But, this trait does not mean that they are incapable of doing what they need to do.

Because these children tend to be less efficient at housework and schoolwork, they may achieve less in academic performance than other children do. Parents and teachers can help children with low persistence and attention span overcome these consequences by various methods.

One way to have a child complete household chores is to divide long tasks into several smaller segments with breaks in between. For example, if the child needs to clean up a messy room, he may feel overwhelmed by what seems to him an enormous task. Break down the job by suggesting that he begin by attacking one small corner; then he can pick up all the clothes; then he can take a break before collecting all the building blocks; and so on, until the job is finally finished.

Homework can be done in much the same way, taking a page or chapter at a time or letting the child read for ten minutes with a brief rest before returning to the work.

Breaking tasks into segments may appear more time-consuming overall; however, it is an effective approach for children with low persistence and attention spans. It allows them to see achievement in small steps and feel more confident that they are making progress. Over time, their persistence can increase as they become more mature and self-motivated.

Your child must be responsible for staying with the task and getting back to it after each break. The objective is completion of the job with sufficient quality, rather than finishing it perfectly by some arbitrary deadline. Try not to hound the child or hover over him. Occasional, gentle reminders may be appropriate. A neutral referee such as a kitchen timer can help him stick to the assignment until the bell rings announcing a short recess.

Your child needs acknowledgment from you that you understand he prefers to dash things off quickly rather than stay on track for long periods. You might express your understanding and support by saying, "Those math problems are difficult, so why don't you give them all you've got for fifteen minutes, then stop for a short break of music before getting back to your homework?"

DISTRACTIBILITY

High The impact of this temperament trait also shifts with age. Distractibility in infancy is largely soothability. When experiencing various forms of distress, such as hunger or fatigue, a highly distractible baby is easily calmed by diversions like rocking, watching a musical mobile, or being picked up and held. It is also important that parents not conclude that the cause of the crying is trivial simply because it stops so quickly.

For older children who are readily distracted, try to reduce the distractions in their environment as much as possible. The television, radio, or CD player should not be turned on where they are doing homework; an out-of-the way place is more conducive to studying than the middle of the family room. Also, younger siblings should not be allowed to interrupt an older one who is trying to study.

For the child who has trouble falling asleep, use room-darkening curtains; turn down the volume of the television; ask that everyone be quieter until she falls asleep; and remove the family pet from her room. Only so many things in the child's immediate environment can be controlled; however, those that cause distractions should be eliminated or reduced within reason.

You may recall from the Introduction that Andy's attention frequently drifted off into space. High distractibility was one of his temperament traits. When this very imaginative boy's attention wandered, his parents and teachers had difficulty bringing his mind back to earth, to the things he was supposed to be doing. When his parents recognized this trait as part and parcel of Andy's temperamental makeup, they accepted it without reprimands or labels. They knew he was not deliberately ignoring or disobeying them; his attention was just easily diverted. They helped Andy by saying such things as "It's hard to keep your attention focused on the history project when there are so many interesting distractions, but this assignment needs to be finished." They also praised him when he did stay with tasks.

When older children are easily distracted, do not blame them; often, they cannot help it. Instead, try to work out strategies to help them get back on track. Ask them for suggestions; they may come up with more creative solutions than you could ever imagine. If you discuss this problem with school-age children, it helps them become more aware of this trait and look for solutions at home and in school.

Being distractible does not necessarily mean that the child will perform poorly. Again, parents can help by avoiding criticism and by praising a rapid return to the task at hand: "It's hard to pay attention to your spelling list when so many things are going on in the classroom, but I see that you're getting back to your work quickly after interruptions." "You are so aware of the world around you that you need to make a special effort to listen carefully to instructions." "It's easy to overlook details or instructions if you don't make a special effort to get them straight from the start."

Low   A crying infant who cannot be rapidly soothed by a distraction is not necessarily in great distress. His temperament may simply not allow him to be calmed as easily by the same methods that work with other babies. These methods can still be tried but are likely to take longer.

Low distractibility is generally an asset for older children because they can ignore noises and other potential interruptions that pull other children away from their schoolwork. But children with this trait may appear unaware of their environment, or they may miss important cues that others notice. Parents and teachers should recognize this low distractibility trait and not interpret it as an intentional failure to obey or heed a call. Be sure to compliment the child for staying with tasks and acknowledge how hard it is to interrupt an interesting activity.

SENSITIVITY

High   Highly sensitive children seem to have more antennae, or more finely tuned antennae, to pick up internal and external stimuli and make fine distinctions between them.

A highly sensitive child may be misunderstood as "finicky" or a "complainer" because he says his collar is too tight, his bed is too hard, or his oatmeal is too lumpy. Such a perceptive child should not be criticized for this quality, rather he should be helped to understand and appreciate this sensitivity. This heightened awareness of stimuli does not necessarily mean that he is more vulnerable to them than other children are. If a sensitive child says that the room is cold, for instance, her comment does not necessarily mean that she is shivering or uncomfortably cold; she may not even need a sweater. She simply is acutely aware of room temperature.

Parents of a highly sensitive child can monitor and adjust environmental stimuli to maximize this child's comfort level. Here is a common example: If a child is having trouble falling asleep, be sure the room is dark, quiet, and comfortable. You might also want to cut out vigorous play, highly competitive games, books with scary stories and pictures, and exciting television programs before bedtime.

Talking to the child about her sensitivity can help her understand it: "You are really aware of what's going on around you." "You seem to react to certain things more than other kids do." "Some things feel funny to you, such as the shirt label at the back of your neck, so why don't we cut off the label and make it more comfortable for you?"

Some children and adults are more sensitive than others are to the feelings and thinking of other people as revealed by their tone of voice, choice of words, facial expressions, and body language. As long as the child's reading of these visual and auditory signals is correct, this sensitivity is almost always an asset and should be encouraged and complimented.

Low   Children with low sensitivity react less to internal and external stimuli; however, this should not be taken to mean that they are unaware of these stimuli or are unfeeling. Because they may be more shielded from external stimuli, such children may need guidance and practice to avoid missing important external cues, such as the sound of an approaching car, a very hot sun, or the frown of a soft-spoken aunt.

Parents can help to make the less sensitive child more conscious of stimuli with statements such as "I guess that scraped elbow must have really hurt more than you let on." "I wonder whether you noticed that somebody is knocking at the door?" "It has cooled off a lot. I'm getting a sweater for myself. Could I get one for you?"

COMMON CLUSTERS OF TEMPERAMENT TRAITS

In Chapter Two we discussed how several traits tend to group together. If your child has the challenging combination of slow approach in initial reaction, low adaptability, high intensity, and negative mood, then review the management suggestions provided previously for each of those traits. If your child is shy or slow to warm up, review the suggestions for slow approach, low adaptability, and negative mood. For the child with what is called "low task orientation," more information is available in Chapter Seven; however, suggestions for dealing with low attention span, high distractibility, and high activity in the previous sections can also apply.

Fortunately, clusters of easy temperament traits are the most common to be found in children. Almost half of any child population studied so far has them. The joys and occasional pitfalls of parenting easy children are examined in this chapter under the headings of regularity, positive initial reaction, high adaptability, low intensity, and positive mood.

A large number of children, about 40 percent, have mixtures of traits that do not place them in any of these clusters. The frequency of these mixtures underscores the importance of thinking of all children in terms of their individual characteristics, rather than trying to lump them into these clusters.

SPECIAL SITUATIONS: NEWBORNS AND ADOLESCENTS

In Chapter One the differences and problems in assessing temperament in these two age ranges are described. Here we discuss how they affect management of newborns and adolescents.

In newborns, the normal variations in behavior are probably largely temporary ones attributable to the influences of pregnancy and the delivery. Nevertheless, they are very real at the time and cannot be ignored. Behaviors most likely to cause parents concern in the first few days and weeks of an infant's life are irritability, low soothability, and irregularity. Strategies mentioned earlier in this chapter, such as those that Jack and Lisa used with Tina, may be helpful. Remember, too, that the professionals involved in a newborn's care—the pediatrician and especially the nurses—should be able to offer some valuable help in recognizing and managing these traits, such as when to pick up, put down, or feed, to settle him down.

Parents can apply the management principles of this chapter—what to do and say in an age-appropriate way—to their teenage children. But adolescents should be taking on increasing amounts of responsibility for their own behaviors and destinies. They should be making more decisions on their own, drawing not only on their peers' opinions but also on resources such as teachers, counselors, and if needed, medical and mental health professionals.

If you helped child to reach a self-understanding of his temperament using the methods discussed earlier in this chapter, then as a teenager he should already be somewhat insightful. If you have not done so, adolescence is not too late to start.

MANAGEMENT BY OTHER PEOPLE

Chapter One described the possibility that your child's temperament might have an impact on other important people in her life—siblings, grandparents, friends, neighbors, teachers—different from the impact it has on you, her parent. This is likely to be a result of the different techniques that others use for getting along with your child. Using many different strategies can be confusing for everyone. How do you make sense of this mixture of responses? First, why not watch how others do it to see what you can learn? What is it about Grandma's quiet handling of tantrums that makes her so successful in quelling them? What does your child's favorite teacher do to lengthen his attention span?

Try to establish a uniform strategy for all to use. In dealing with Joe's sensitivity, you can take Uncle George aside and ask him not to criticize Joe for "acting like an old lady" because he notices variations in the feel and smell of things. Explain what you have learned about sensitivity and try to enlist Uncle George's help in reassuring Joe that it is okay to be sensitive to these stimuli.

At parent–teacher conferences, discuss what you know about your child's temperament with teachers, and let them know what management techniques work well at home. Ask them about their observations of your child's temperament, and inquire about strategies they find effective.

OTHER ASPECTS OF MANAGEMENT

What about the physical, rather than behavioral management of temperament? The news media today are full of reports about dangerous influences on children's intelligence and behavior from foods and environmental toxins. Unquestionably, a person's nutritional state is important; children who are malnourished do not function well. Yet the frightening reports of dangers of food additives, colorings, and sugar have not stood up to scientific testing. Even so, that does not rule out the possibility that rare individuals may have unique sensitivities, or that some substances may yet be confirmed as troublesome for many children.

Environmental toxins are an increasing source of concern to health authorities. The dangers posed by lead poisoning to children's thinking and behavior are well established, and worldwide efforts are attempting to eradicate this menace. Other substances such as PCBs, certain pesticides, and heavy metals are under intense scrutiny by public health officials. For now, the only sensible general plan for families is to avoid ingestion and inhalation of any of the substances under reasonable suspicion.

Some standard medications given for a variety of ailments may influence a child's behavior. Common drugs to look out for are phenobarbital, theophylline, antihistamines, and cortisonelike medications. Discuss with the psysician whether such drugs may be influencing your child's temperament or other behavior. If so, the drug dosage can be changed or a different drug can be prescribed.

The complicated issue of the use of medications such as methylphenidate (Ritalin) for managing temperament is discussed at length in Chapter Seven.

ADDITIONAL RESOURCES FOR MANAGING TEMPERAMENT

Some communities like Minneapolis, Minnesota; Philadelphia and West Chester, Pennsylvania; New York City; LaGrande, Oregon; Vancouver, British Columbia; and areas of California are fortunate to have experts who may be able to provide and individualize information about temperament for you (see Professional Advisors in the Resources section at the end of this book). However, most locations have limited resources. If you are interested in starting a parent information and support group in your area, please turn to the Resources section where parent resource groups are listed.

If your child's situation is further complicated by a behavioral problem, in addition to temperament issues, the next chapter should be useful to you.

The following table summarizes the main points discussed in this chapter regarding management of the high and low ends of the nine temperament characteristics. It is provided as a quick reference for any future occasion when your child encounters new situations and when you may want to refresh your knowledge and skills. In each case, when talking about or with your child, remember to substitute more neutral descriptions for critical labels; for example, use the word "energetic" instead of "hyper" or "wild."

SUMMARY OF MANAGEMENT APPROACHES

HIGH ACTIVITY	LOW ACTIVITY
Help the child find ample opportunity for physical activity. Avoid unnecessary restrictions of activity. Demand restraint of motion appropriate for age when necessary.	Allow extra time to complete tasks. Set realistic limits, such as meeting the school bus on time. Do not criticize slow speed.
HIGH REGULARITY	LOW REGULARITY
In an infant, plan feedings and other activities on a schedule. In an older child, advise of expected disruptions of the schedule.	In an infant, first try to accommodate the preference for irregularity, then gradually steer her toward a more regular schedule. An older child can be expected increasingly to regularize his eating and sleeping times, even if he does not feel hungry or sleepy on schedule.

(continued)	
APPROACHING OR BOLD INITIAL REACTION	**WITHDRAWING OR INHIBITED INITIAL REACTION**
Reinforce with praise if positive. Remember that the initial positive reaction may not last. Be aware of the child's boldness in dangerous situations.	Avoid overload of new experiences. Prepare the child for new situations and introduce her to them slowly. Do not push too hard. Praise her for overcoming her fears of novelty. Encourage self-management as the child grows older.
HIGH ADAPTABILITY	**LOW ADAPTABILITY**
Look out for possible susceptibility to unfavorable influences in school and elsewhere.	Avoid unnecessary requirements to adapt. Reduce or spread out necessary adaptations, arranging for gradual changes in stages. Do not push too hard or too quickly. Give advance warnings about what to expect. Teach social skills to expedite adaptation. Maintain reasonable expectations for change. Support and praise effort.
HIGH INTENSITY	**LOW INTENSITY**
Intensity may exaggerate the apparent importance of response. Avoid reacting to the child with the same intensity; try to read the child's real need and respond calmly to that need. Do not give in just to make peace. Enjoy intense positive responses.	Try to read the child's real need, and do not mistake it as trivial just because it is mildly expressed. Take complaints seriously.

POSITIVE MOOD	NEGATIVE MOOD
Encourage positive and friendly responses. Look out only for those situations in which your child's outward positive behavior may mask true distress, such as with pain, and situations in which being too friendly may be troublesome, such as with strangers.	Remember that it is just your child's style, unless there is an underlying behavioral or emotional problem. Do not let the child's mood make you feel guilty or angry; his mood is not your fault. Ignore as many of the glum, unfriendly responses as possible; however, try to spot and deal with the real distress. Advise an older child to try harder to be pleasant with people.
HIGH PERSISTENCE AND ATTENTION SPAN	LOW PERSISTENCE AND ATTENTION SPAN
Redirect a persistent toddler whose persistence is annoying. In an older child, warn about the need to end or interrupt activity when continued for too long. Reassure the child that leaving some tasks unfinished is acceptable.	The child may need help organizing tasks into shorter segments with periodic breaks; however, the responsibility for completion of the task belongs with the child. Reward the adequate completion of the task and not the speed with which it is done.
HIGH DISTRACTIBILITY	LOW DISTRACTIBILITY
If the problem involves an older child, try to eliminate or reduce competing stimuli. Gently redirect the child to the task at hand when necessary; however, encourage the child to assume his own responsibility for doing this. Praise adequately for completing the task.	If the child ignores necessary interruptions, do not assume it is deliberate disobedience.

(continued)	
HIGH SENSITIVITY	LOW SENSITIVITY
Avoid excessive stimulation. Eliminate stimuli if disruptive. Avoid overestimating extreme responses to stimuli. Help the older child understand this trait in himself. Support and encourage the child's sensitivity to the feelings of others.	Look out for underreporting of pain and other distress. Help the child develop an awareness of important internal and external stimuli.

CHAPTER FOUR

Behavioral Problems and Temperament

Meet Chad, aged 4, Sandra and Rick Jordan's first child. A happy, healthy boy, Chad was nurtured and adored by parents who handled his behavior quite successfully. Sandra and Rick understood Chad's temperament. He tended to withdraw or warm up slowly in new situations. His reactions tended to be intense and were often rather negative. He did not adapt easily to novelty. He preferred set routines and usually became upset if anything intruded, such as a last-minute change in plans, a substitute's filling in for his favorite nursery school teacher, or a visit from his parents' friends that disrupted his bath and bedtime schedule.

Sandra and Rick were able to achieve a good fit between Chad's temperament and their parenting approach because they accurately gauged their son's temperament. They accepted it as both normal and unique to him, and they adjusted their own expectations and responses to match his temperament. Chad's parents used some of the methods suggested in Chapter Three for children whose temperament characteristics are similar to their son's. Overall, Chad was a well-adjusted child with no behavioral problems. Just a bit feisty.

But that is not a happily-ever-after ending. The Jordans had a second child soon after Chad's fourth birthday. Rick's job also changed, and it kept him away from home longer and more frequently. Chad's behavior changed, too. He clearly did not appreciate the new interloper in the bassinet.

He grew angry and aggressive, dumping bowls of soggy cereal on the floor, hitting the cat, and running out of the room when Sandra made simple requests such as "It's time to get dressed." One morning Sandra walked into the baby's room to discover Chad scribbling on the wall with marking pens.

Sandra and Rick had known that Chad had some temperament traits that could be challenging, and they had managed them fairly well until now. Chad's new behaviors appeared unexpectedly and at a difficult time in their lives. Sandra was exhausted by the added responsibilities of a new baby, and she felt unsupported by Rick because he was often absent from home. Increasingly impatient with Chad, she had reacted to his negative behaviors with shouting and punishments: "Time out! In your room for one hour! No bedtime story for you!" Her overreaction, which was a side of her that Chad had never experienced before, only made him more rebellious and disobedient.

Rick returned one evening from a business trip to find Sandra red-eyed and discouraged. They decided that they needed to figure out a better way to handle Chad. The next night, after both children had fallen asleep, Sandra and Rick had a long discussion about the problem and concluded that Chad had not turned into a little monster. There was no mysterious, underlying cause that would lead to lifelong problems. He was not suffering any psychological damage. Chad was just overreacting to the new baby and to the changes in parental care.

The Jordans realized that it was not unusual for a child with Chad's temperament to react dramatically to a rather common situation such as a new baby in the family. This infant was an intruder in a home where Chad had reigned as an only child and was very much the center of attention.

The baby upset the balance in Chad's life, stole his parents'
time and attention, and brought about changes in household
routines and in Chad's relations with his parents.

An event such as the arrival of a new sibling would be better
accepted by a child whose temperament was more easygoing and
open to change. Such an event can overwhelm a child with Chad's
temperament. Add to that his mother's unhelpful reactions and his
father's increasing absence, and it is not surprising that Chad displayed anger and aggression.

Knowing Chad's temperament helped to explain his behavior.
That knowledge then guided Sandra and Rick in helping him adjust
more successfully to a new environment that included a little brother.
They decided that they needed to set limits on Chad's behavior while
simultaneously taking into account his temperament traits. They
made an effort to spend more time alone with Chad, and they used
behavioral modification techniques to teach him that his actions had
consequences. If he spilled cereal, he had to clean it up. If he did not
put his cars and trucks away before bedtime, he was not allowed to
play with them the next morning.

Chad's parents also praised his efforts and achievements. They
began to involve him in activities with the baby, such as pushing the
carriage when they went for a walk. They gave him special "big
brother" jobs that made him feel responsible and important. They
introduced these opportunities slowly and gently, however, because
they knew that Chad adapted only gradually to changes. By recognizing their son's unique temperament and tailoring their responses
accordingly, Sandra and Rick were able to steer Chad back to normal
behavior and head off further behavioral problems. And that is a
principal goal of this book: to enable parents to take steps toward
better understanding and stress reduction in interactions with their
children.

BEHAVIORAL ADJUSTMENT VERSUS TEMPERAMENT

Before dealing with behavioral problems related to temperament, it is first necessary to clarify the difference between the two. Behavioral adjustment refers to what the child does: scribbling on walls, deliberately spilling cereal, defying a parent. Temperament determines how the child reacts to change or stress. In Chad's case, his low adaptability and tendency to react intensely and negatively were how he reacted to change (a new baby brother) and other stressors (the increased absence of his father and the fatigue and impatience of his mother). These temperament traits made it difficult for him to welcome a new sibling and accept disruptions in the family's routine, and they were played out in Chad's angry and aggressive behavior.

The term *behavioral adjustment* is considered to have two dimensions: external and internal. It refers to how well a child functions externally, or her observable behavior both in relationships with people and in the performance of tasks. It also refers to how well a child functions internally in terms her of self-relations, thinking, and feeling. Success in these areas of adjustment can be measured in fairly simple ways.

Success in behavioral adjustment is measured by social relations, task performance, self-relations, internal status, and coping style. All of these measures of behavioral adjustment concern the *content* and substance of behavior, rather than the *style*. Temperament and adjustment influence each other; nonetheless, making this distinction is very important.

SOCIAL RELATIONS

Does your child's behavior show social competence or poor social skills? How does he get along with other people? Problems in this area involve behavior that is aggressive toward people or property, such as bullying, cruelty, fighting, and stealing; oppositional, defiant, disagreeable behavior, such as being consistently very argumentative and noncompliant with parents' requests; or other evidence of failure to learn basic social skills, such as selfishness or bad manners.

TASK PERFORMANCE

To what extent does your child work and play up to reasonable expectations for her age or underachieve according to the same measure? School is the main arena in which task performance is rated; however, accomplishments or deficits at home and in the community should also be considered.

SELF-RELATIONS

Does your child possess self-assurance, or is he deficient in self-regard, self-care, or self-regulation? The answers to these questions are the measures used in this area of adjustment. Problems may include poor self-esteem, self-neglect, impulsiveness, or excessive self-restraint.

INTERNAL STATUS

Is there general personal contentment, or are there disturbances in thinking, feeling, or bodily functions? Problems of internal status are anxiety, depression, phobias, obsessions, and compulsions; sleeping, eating, and bowel and bladder dysfunctions; and unexplained recurring pains.

COPING STYLE

How effective or ineffective is your child's overall pattern of dealing with life's stressors? Coping style seems to be made up of temperament, intelligence, experience, and other factors.

INTERACTION BETWEEN TEMPERAMENT AND BEHAVIORAL ADJUSTMENT

What do we know about the relationship of temperament to the areas of behavioral adjustment mentioned previously? Children's behavioral disorders are generally thought to stem from three main problem areas: the child, family, and physical and social world outside the family.

Factors in the child herself include disorders of the nervous system, such as developmental and learning disabilities, and chronic or recurrent physical illness. Undesirable family influences are well known, for example, parental discord, abuse, and neglect. Unfavorable forces outside the home may include school, neighborhood, and wider community factors such as poverty and violence. All of these are important contributors to children's behavioral adjustment.

Less recognized—and a central point of this book—is the fact that behavioral problems can also emerge when there is a poor fit between a child's temperament and her parents' child care practices, both of which may be quite normal. This fact is too often overlooked by both professionals and families.

Temperament can be a partial cause of a behavioral problem when it conflicts with the values and expectations of parents or other care givers. The stress and conflict produced by this poor fit may result in the adjustment problem. Some previous abnormal condition in either the child, such as a disability, or in the parent, such as depression, may also exist; however, an abnormal condition does not have to be present and often is not.

In a classic research study, which began in 1956 and followed children from infancy into adulthood, Chess and Thomas demonstrated that in the first twelve years of life, a child with any kind of temperament pattern could develop a behavioral problem. Yet they found that children most likely to display behavioral disorders had the temperament characteristics of low adaptability, withdrawing ini-tial reaction, negative mood, high intensity, and to a lesser extent, irregularity. These challenging children (Chess and Thomas called them "difficult") and "slow to warm up" youngsters were most likely to generate friction with their parents and had the highest rate of behavioral problems.

When their parents did not reduce the stress by improving the fit, these children responded with their available coping strategies, and an adjustment disturbance tended to arise if they did not succeed. Numerous other investigators have come up with similar results with different population samples.

COMMON PROBLEMS

What are the most common behavioral problems that spring from a poor fit between a child's temperament and the environment, espe-cially parents' child care strategies? Several studies, including one of my own, have attempted to answer this question. A few years ago, I reviewed more than one thousand patient charts from my pediatric practice and discovered three principal forms of behavioral problems related to temperament interactions:

- Acute social behavioral problems were frequently exhibited by children with challenging temperaments who had been doing satisfactorily under normal circumstances with com-petent parental handling but who, like Chad, reacted to suddenly increased stress more dramatically than other children—siblings or classmates—who tolerated the stress without such disruption.

- School problems.

- Recurring behavioral problems arose as separate episodes of behavioral disturbance with normal periods between them.

Recurring behavioral problems are generally less sudden and dramatic than an eruption of behavior such as that of Chad. Whereas a child's temperament may remain somewhat the same, these behavioral problems come and go. Changing external circumstances alter the fit between those circumstances and the child's behavioral style, giving rise to new problems of interaction.

Throughout her early years Emily was an irritable, inflexible, sensitive child. Despite these traits, she had behavioral problems only during short, intermittent periods. During her first weeks, Emily cried excessively until her parents eventually discovered the importance of not being overly responsive to such a sensitive baby. By eight months of age, her temperament characteristics and her parents' tendency to be overattentive had led to another problem, frequent night awakenings. Again, they realized the importance of shaping their responses to her real needs. They read a book about sleep problems and devised a plan to withdraw their nighttime involvement. They did so gradually by tapering off and finally stopping the night feedings and by shortening and then ceasing their visits to her crib. They let her develop self-soothing skills.

While her parents' change of response solved that problem, Emily's temperament did not change. As she grew older, it clashed from time to time with various circumstances. When she was two years old, her mother took her by the hand to enroll her at a local day care center. On their way into the building, Emily pulled away from her mother with such force that her elbow joint was partially dislocated. The elbow was easily restored to its normal position by her doctor, but the day care teacher told her mother, "Emily may not be ready for day care yet."

Despite her sensitivity, irritability, and inflexibility, Emily was a generally well-adjusted child. She had the endearing qualities of a contagious laugh and an affectionate way with friends and family that made her well liked by others. As her parents came to understand her temperament, they helped her to cope less explosively and more effectively with various adversities as they arose. And as she became better able to handle such challenges, the frequency of these troubling episodes decreased.

It is important to recognize that temperament helps to promote behavioral adjustment as well as behavioral problems. When temperament meets novelty or challenge, the outcome depends on the fit between those circumstances and the child's temperament. The same persistence that causes one child to be abused by an overstressed parent may cause a similar child to excel in accomplishing new physical or intellectual skills when the circumstances are right. The same low adaptability that infuriates a parent seeking to accomplish rapid toilet training may protect another child (or even the same one) from future harm by making him less susceptible to the allure of drugs and other dangers present in the neighborhood.

WHAT TO DO

This book is not intended to advise parents about management of all kinds of behavioral problems. Some are too complex, chronic, or severe for parents' efforts to solve them without the help of appropriate professionals. But, many behavioral problems associated with basically normal children are simple, transient, and only mild to moderate in severity, and they can be dealt with effectively by parents. Problems involving temperament interactions especially lend themselves to resolution by the family.

The following sections should help to enhance your understanding of behavioral concerns. When those problems are related to temperament interactions, steps toward solutions are suggested.

CLARIFY THE CONCERN

The first step is to focus on the behavior that concerns you by asking yourself the following questions:

What is the problem?

What does it consist of?

How often does it occur?

How long does it last?

How severe is it?

How much does it bother you?

How much does it bother teachers and other children?

What improves the behavior?

What makes it worse?

The answers to these questions probably will become clearer if you write down your concerns in the notebook you used earlier. Perhaps some of the same behavioral problems that are now confounding you were included in the notes you took when identifying your child's temperament.

A key to clarifying the concern is understanding the general nature of the behavior that bothers you. There are four possible explanations.

- With a behavioral adjustment problem, there should be some disturbance in one of the areas listed earlier in this chapter, such as social relations, task performance, self-relations, internal status, or coping style.

- When you cannot conclude for certain that there is an ongoing problem in one or more of those areas, perhaps your child's temperament itself is troubling you. This is quite common. You should be able to recognize this is so from the descriptions in Chapter Three, and the suggestions about management included there should provide a useful guide to dealing with those concerns.

- Whatever you are finding difficult to handle may be a combination of temperament and a resulting behavioral adjustment problem. In that case, you will have identified both challenging temperament traits and areas of adjustment problems.

- On your own or with the help of friends, relatives, or professional advisors, you may decide that the seemingly problematic behavior is actually normal and average. It may only seem abnormal because of your inexperience as parents or because various personal stresses have distorted your judgment or perspective.

SET OBJECTIVES

Can I handle it? The next step is to ask whether you can realistically solve this problem yourself, or whether you need the help of a psychologist or psychiatrist. What does your child need? Who can best provide what is needed? The answers may not be clear at this point. If you are unsure, discuss your problem with your child's physician. You should reach out for professional help right away if the behavioral problem is severe, that is, if it poses potential harm to your child or others; if it is chronic, that is, ongoing for more than the past few weeks; or if it is complex, that is, problems in more than one area, such as sleep disturbance coupled with school avoidance.

The problem may be related to upsetting family or social circumstances, such as a divorce, a recent experience of abuse, the death of a close relative or friend, or a frightening experience with violence. Under any of these circumstances parents often are too distressed themselves to be able to provide necessary impartial guidance. Do not hesitate to seek help.

What does that leave for parents to do on their own? Most minor behavioral problems, and some moderately severe ones, involve temperament interactions: The child's temperament clashes with whatever is going on in her life at the moment. If you feel reasonably certain that this is your child's situation, first try to handle it yourself. See what you can do to improve the fit by altering those circumstances that are colliding with your child's temperament. If matters do not improve in a few weeks, you can turn to professional assistance. Meanwhile, try to continue this approach while waiting for your appointment.

EVALUATE THE BEHAVIOR

Where does the problem come from? This step requires you to decide whether a relationship exists between the behavioral problem that you have just clarified and your child's temperament as you profiled it. The simplest way to assess this relationship is to ask yourself, your spouse, or another adult who knows your child well whether the problem seems to involve a poor fit because you are reacting inappropriately to your child's temperament. For instance, could your overattention to your baby's irritability be responsible for her being more wakeful at night? Could your pushing your shy child too hard and too fast be the cause of his resistance to getting out of the car and walking into school? Could your child's rebellion against the new second-grade teacher stem from her demands that all children adjust to her rigid program?

We return to Chad. His parents followed the first three steps described in the subsequent sections. They decided which annoying behaviors they wanted to eliminate: his aggression and noncompliance. In determining their goals, they decided that they probably could handle this without professional intervention because it was not likely to be a major disturbance. In evaluating his behavior more extensively, Sandra and Rick reminded themselves of Chad's temperament patterns with which they were well acquainted. They concluded that his behavioral problems could be traced to the inter-action between his temperament and the stressful situation at home, which was a combination of a new baby, weakened support from Rick's absence, and an exhausted Sandra. The final step was a plan of management.

PLAN A SOLUTION

What should I do? By now you have determined that your child has a behavioral problem that is most likely attributable to a temperament–parenting mismatch. At this point, you are feeling confident about trying to work out the solution on your own without professional help. Your resolution can be outlined by the following plan.

Improve the fit to reduce the stress

If the friction between you and your child's temperament has led to the undesirable behavior, the first step is to find ways to reduce the unnecessary part of that stress. You should be looking for different ways of interacting with your child, ways that are more comfortable for both of you but that do not sacrifice the main objectives of behavioral adjustment, such as social competence and task performance. For example, if the problem centers around your child refusing to do his homework and you have been engaged in a shouting match with him, the solution is not to deal with the stress by withdrawing and letting him off the hook. Doing so may reduce the stress but will not help his task performance.

You should not surrender your authority; simply try to find more congenial ways of enforcing it. Look for alternate pathways to reach the same goals. Successful changes both reduce the friction and stress and improve or eliminate the problem. On the homework battle-ground, for instance, a parent might lower her voice a few decibels, take a deep breath, and start over in a calmer tone: "Okay, Billy. I know you hate copying your spelling words over and over again. It is a drag, I admit, but it needs to be done tonight. So why don't you take a five-minute break? Then come back and finish up, and I'll stay out of your hair."

In Chad's case, his parents could not change their situation. Sandra was still busy with the demands of baby care, and Rick had to meet the performance requirements of his company. But they could modify their interaction with Chad: They improved the fit and reduced stress by stopping their overreactions to his own overreacting.

Manage your child's temperament with greater understanding and tolerance

When working your way through a behavioral problem, it is easy to focus too narrowly on that specific conflict of the moment. You may find great help in stepping back and looking at the bigger picture. You may want to review with your spouse, or another adult who knows your child well, some other ways your child's temperament is affecting your life. Perhaps you are being too lenient or too strict about these behaviors. Someone else's perspective can help you crystallize your own thinking.

Chapter Three presented some strategies to guide you in this review process. The goal is to gain a better insight into your general relationship with your child so that you can avoid similar crises in the future. This insight will help you recognize what is happening, and why, when a new problem surfaces, and it can make that next conflict as brief as possible.

Use other measures of general behavioral management

In addition to improving the fit, you may need to use other techniques to guide your child back to more normal functioning. Other factors may be contributing to the problem: perhaps a physical illness, a developmental disability, or some unfavorable environmental influences. You should seek help if your personal problems are getting in the way of your own satisfactory functioning as a parent; for example, a separation or divorce proceeding may be consuming all your energy and attention. Any harmful force, such as family dysfunction (for example, parents' fighting), neighborhood violence, or frightening television programs, must be dealt with by parents.

Some of the established methods of behavioral management may be necessary. Discipline teaches children acceptable behavior. It helps them develop social skills, a conscience, and self-esteem. Its primary elements are positive reinforcement and other strategies such as time-out and denial of privileges. Punishment, mainly unpleasant verbal or physical actions, may discourage unacceptable behavior; however, it does not teach acceptable, appropriate behavior and can lower self-esteem. These measures are not the central focus of this book but are discussed at length in other books on child rearing (see Resources).

Chad's parents not only correctly figured out the nature of the problem with their son's behavior, they considered ways to avoid future problems and took the necessary steps for behavioral management. They called for "time-in" for him to have their undivided attention. They praised his good behavior, but they also made him face the consequences of his unacceptable actions, such as cleaning up his own spills.

Get help

If you feel that you are in over your head with a problem, either at the outset or after having tried the steps listed previously, reach for assistance from a mental health professional. Your pediatrician or family doctor may be able to help you, but usually the services of a child psychologist or psychiatrist are needed. This is a difficult move for most people to make because it is unfamiliar.

The situation can be further complicated due to the ignorance of many mental health professionals with regard to temperament differences and how best to handle them. Their advice will probably be less helpful. Your family physician or pediatrician should be a good person to ask first for recommendations.

Assistance comes in other forms as well. Books, tapes, lectures, parent support groups, and friends may also contribute perspective and wisdom. If you have received recommendations for therapies that seem odd or too unfamiliar to you, valuable sources for obtaining an authoritative evaluation are the following:

- American Academy of Pediatrics
  P.O. Box 927
  Elk Grove Village, IL 60009-0927
  Telephone: 847-228-5005

- American Academy of Child and Adolescent Psychiatry
  3615 Wisconsin Avenue NW
  Washington, DC 20016
  Telephone: 202-966-7300

- American Psychological Association
  750 First Street NE
  Washington, DC 20002
  Telephone: 202-336-5500

THE OUTCOME

How likely is it that this strategy will succeed? At present, we cannot say for certain because research into temperament differences and their impact on behavior is only a generation old; however, early results are certainly encouraging. Interest in the subject is high, the research is expanding, and both are expected to continue.

In the New York Longitudinal Study, conducted by Chess and Thomas, most children with behavioral problems were found to do much better after two or three counseling sessions with a child psychiatrist, especially when several factors were present:

The problems were of recent onset and not highly complex.

The parents were informed, stable, and cooperative.

The areas of disharmony in the fit were fairly obvious.

What do we know about the success of parents who are doing much of the same problem-solving on their own? Unfortunately, we have no data on this. Adequate surveys have yet to be performed. Parents who are successful do not walk into the offices of professionals and are not counted in evaluation studies. Nevertheless, a great deal of anecdotal evidence gives the definite impression that parents frequently do very well at this task. Successful outcomes occur often enough that it seems reasonable to recommend that you apply your own knowledge and skills when the problem is fairly simple, recent, and neither dangerous nor harmful—physically or emotionally—to the child or someone else.

CHAPTER FIVE

Temperament's Impact on Normal Development and Disabilities

In medicine and psychology, the term *development* refers to the evolution of new abilities as the central nervous system matures. As children grow, their nervous systems allow them to develop increasingly elaborate gross and fine motor skills, speech and language, and social skills. *Developmental disabilities* is a term referring to the disturbances of function in these areas that result from an impairment of the nervous system.

NORMAL DEVELOPMENT

Parents observe the developmental process by milestones, that is, the emergence of new skills that are awaited expectantly and greeted with great joy; for example, when she first crawls, sits without support, stands alone, takes a step, says a word, feeds herself with a spoon, catches a ball, learns to read, holds a pencil, writes her name, and so on. Along with other factors, individual temperament traits can influence the rate of a child's development. Development will advance best when temperament traits encourage and enable a child to get the most out of her present abilities and the resources in her environment and when the environment is appropriately stimulating and responsive.

When Ian started to walk, his very active temperament fueled his new skill. He took off and was soon walking all around the house. He practiced this new skill energetically until he walked so steadily and quickly that he soon discovered the next steps, climbing and running.

Danny, whose temperament is less active, pulled himself to a stand at the same age as Ian, but Danny was less interested in stepping out on his own. He was perfectly content to sit still, amusing himself with toys that were within reach. When Danny did take his first independent steps, he did not walk far or often. He toddled deliberately from place to place to get whatever he wanted at the moment, but he was not interested in walking for its own sake.

There was nothing wrong with Danny's development. It occurred within a normal range for his age. Eventually he ran, skipped, jumped, and learned to ride a bike, usually when he wanted to join other children in these activities, rather than just for the fun of it.

Temperament directly affects how infants and toddlers use their emerging developmental skills and capabilities, as the differences between Ian and Danny's activity traits show. Even before he could walk, Ian's active temperament pushed him to explore his environment vigorously. He scooted around the kitchen floor on hands and knees, opened cupboard doors and drawers, and pulled himself up to a standing position at the coffee table so he could reach a glittering glass vase of flowers. Ian's active temperament would have helped him to progress well in any environment.

Temperament also affects development indirectly by selecting or evoking from the environment experiences that are useful for development.

Ian's older sister, Mandy, is more socially outgoing than Ian. When she learned to talk, she became a quite a chatterbox. She questioned relatives, neighbors, shopkeepers, and bus drivers, talking to everyone within earshot whether or not she knew the person. Her readiness to start conversations sparked her language abilities. The more she chatted, the more people talked to her. Her pleasant, approaching, adaptable temperament evoked stimulating feedback from those around her. She heard, absorbed, and used increasingly sophisticated language. Ian did not adjust to new social situations as easily. Even though he began to speak at about the same age as his sister, he was—and still is—more reserved around other people. He speaks in shorter phrases and with a more limited vocabulary and simpler sentence structure. There is nothing wrong with Ian's verbal or cognitive abilities; however, he acquired language skills more slowly than Mandy because Ian did not take advantage of opportunities to talk as much as she did.

Throughout his early years, Ian also proved to be quite persistent as well as active. When a toy was too high to reach, he groped for it unsuccessfully, but did not give up. After several failed attempts, he would push a chair to the right spot and climb up to get the toy. Ian also spent hours absorbed in doing puzzles and constructing tall towers of blocks. If the blocks fell down, he simply rebuilt the tower. If the puzzle pieces did not fit together, he stuck with a trial-and-error approach until he found the right combination. Ian's persistence was a considerable asset at this stage of his development, although his mother found his extensive exploration of the kitchen cabinets a bit trying.

When he was older, this persistence trait stood him well as he was able to work diligently for hours on homework projects. In other words, Ian's temperament remained constant (persistent, active, somewhat shy) throughout infancy and childhood but was applied differently to, and influenced, each developmental stage as he mastered it and moved on to the next level.

Parents of infants and toddlers who exhibit the more challenging temperament traits—irregularity, intensity, slow initial acceptance, low adaptability, negative mood—should not be discouraged. These characteristics do not necessarily mean the child's development will be slow. Although these traits can be somewhat difficult to live with day to day, when a child is handled well by understanding and imaginative parents his development can be normal or even above average.

Consider Lily, a child who does not adapt easily to changes in her routine and who is quite active, persistent, and intense. Lily enjoys playing outdoors and does so almost every day. On a rainy day, however, she stubbornly insists that a trip to the playground to practice riding her two-wheeler is absolutely essential to her survival. She does not accept rational explanations from her parents. Her intense lobbying often drives them to the nearest headache remedy.

Then they think of it this way: Lily is also practicing cognitive and verbal skills as she tries to convince them to get their raincoats and go outside. Of course, Lily's parents do not have to give in to her loud, persistent demands. Despite its downside, this situation can be viewed as an opportunity for Lily's growth and development instead of a battle of wills.

You may ask how Lily's parents accomplish this. They let her express her request but suggest that she do so in a softer voice: "My ears hear you better if you speak more quietly. Thank you." They let her verbalize her reasons and let her know that they have really listened and considered her request: "I know how much you want to play outdoors. It probably would be more fun than staying inside." While letting her know that her wish is unacceptable at the moment, they give her a graceful way out: "We cannot go to the playground until the rain stops. So for now, would you like to play a board game or help me do some baking?"

Giving Lily the choice of alternative activities does not put her down, as would a comment such as "Can't you see it's raining? Of course, you can't go outside!" Instead, it lets her know that she has been heard, which reinforces her new verbal and cognitive skills and gives her the opportunity to think about and express how this dilemma might be resolved in another way. Providing this choice not only gently nudges her development to the next level, but also improves the fit between her temperament and the situation. And it does not make her more demanding.

In school-age children, the traits that influence development most strongly are persistence, attention span, and adaptability. (Temperament and school issues are discussed in Chapter Seven.) A child's low persistence may frustrate parents and teachers; however, they should not become too discouraged. As they try to guide such a child through schoolwork, they can take encouragement from the example of the Irish poet William Butler Yeats, who confesses in his autobiography, "Because I had found it hard to attend to anything less interesting than my thoughts, I was difficult to teach. . . . I was much older than children who read easily. . . . [As a result, uncles and aunts who had tried to teach him] had come to think, as I have learnt since, that I had not all my faculties." Of course, not only did Yeats learn to read, but he became what many consider to be the greatest poet to write in English in the twentieth century.

Even in disadvantaged or unfavorable settings—amid poverty, neglect, high stress at home, or other adverse conditions—children with certain temperament traits seem to progress and even thrive developmentally because these traits protect them against adversity. Research has shown those protective traits to include high activity, positive mood, high adaptability, and persistence. As with behavioral adjustment, a child's developmental progress depends on the fit between his traits and whatever the environment offers. With a good fit, development moves along faster.

How much difference does temperament make? There is clear research evidence that these effects are felt within the normal range of development, but nothing in the research suggests that temperament can pull a child below the normal level or push him up into the superior range of development.

THE ROLE OF TEMPERAMENT IN DEVELOPMENTAL DISABILITIES

Children with developmental disabilities have inborn temperaments just like their nondisabled brothers and sisters. Recent studies have found that, except in cases of brain injury, children with disabilities have few differences in temperament from other children. Children with disabilities have the same nine traits, some of which are more prominent than others, as is true with all children. Some are shy, while others are outgoing; some are stubborn, while others are flexible. In all cases, those temperament characteristics influence the child's development, behavior, and care.

Specific disabilities, such as cerebral palsy or deafness, are apparently not accompanied by distinctive temperament patterns or styles. This was first shown by the research that questioned the traditional view that all children with Down syndrome have mild, pleasant temperaments. Investigations are under way to consider Klinefelter's, Turner's, Williams, and fragile X syndromes and possible genetic connections with temperament patterns. Consistent patterns have not yet emerged, but, with further studies, they may. For example, some reports say that children with Klinefelter's syndrome are rather shy.

For many years, children with Down syndrome—the most commonly identified type of mental retardation and the type most frequently studied by researchers—were believed to have very pleasant, placid temperaments. This textbook stereotype undoubtedly grew out of a general observation that their below-normal intelligence did not challenge rules and regulations, and therefore, they were less disruptive and disobedient. Most were slower in motor development than were children without disabilities, a fact their parents may have appreciated during the early years because as toddlers they got into less trouble, such as climbing out of their cribs or up onto counter-tops. This lower mobility contributed to the "easy" temperament label. The delayed verbal skills of these children may have led some to believe that they were satisfied because they did not complain very much.

In recent years, however, that stereotype has crumbled. Today's research is based on children who are reared at home rather than in custodial institutions, and many of these children are enrolled in early intervention programs that foster their physical, social, and cognitive development. Many children with disabilities are now included in regular school programs when they reach school age, rather than being segregated in special education classrooms for the entire school day. As a result, parents and professionals have begun to see these children as individuals with distinct personalities, abilities, and, yes, temperaments. In fact, in the last twenty-five years, several formal studies of their temperaments have usually revealed a typical normal range.

As with the child without a disability, some temperament characteristics are particularly useful for any child with a disability or developmental delay. A positive mood should be an obvious plus in living with a disability. High adaptability is another advantage. For a child whose condition requires intensive therapies, adaptability and persistence can make this arduous process easier to tolerate and are likely to increase the therapy's success. The opposite traits may slow the pace of therapy. An example follows.

In an early intervention program, teachers are preparing Janet, a nine-month-old baby with Down syndrome, to stand alone as a prerequisite for walking. They pull her gently from a sitting to an upright position so that she will bear weight on her feet. The goal is to prepare her leg muscles to support her in a standing position and to help her develop the balance necessary to take steps.

Janet does not adapt easily to this new exercise. She registers her dislike by pulling her legs up in a froglike-style instead of straightening her legs and putting her feet on the floor. Her parents and teachers recognize that she adapts slowly to new activities and repeat the standing exercise several times over the next few days until Janet accepts it. Her development—in this case, walking—is delayed somewhat longer than another child of the same age, who also has Down syndrome and is enrolled in the same early intervention program, but who has a more adaptable temperament. The teachers helped Janet's parents recognize that low adaptability is neither a part of Down syndrome nor something they have done wrong. It is simply a part of Janet's temperament.

What about behavioral problems in children with disabilities? In Chess and Thomas's New York Longitudinal Study, a group of fifty-two children, aged 5 to 12 years, with mental retardation, living in middle-class homes, did not differ noticeably from children without disabilities of the same ages as to the frequency of the "difficult" temperament traits. One relationship was noted, however. When children were both mentally retarded and had these characteristics, their parents had more trouble managing them and they were more likely to have behavioral disorders than if the children were only difficult or developmentally normal. In other words, the disability adds to the challenging temperament and vice versa; children with both are more likely to have behavioral problems than those with either alone.

Two recent reviews of all the studies of behavioral problems in children with developmental disabilities came to the same conclusion. Furthermore, temperaments play a larger role than does the nature or severity of the disability. When children with developmental delays or disabilities do have behavioral problems, they have them for the same reasons as do children without disabilities. If a child has a cluster of challenging temperament traits, and the adults in his life do not alter their interaction and the environment to produce a better fit, then that child is more likely to have behavioral problems, whether or not he has a disability.

WHAT PARENTS CAN DO

Families of children with developmental delays face more emotional, financial, and physical challenges than other families do. If you are the parent of a child with a disability, your calendar is undoubtedly full of doctors' appointments, teacher conferences, and therapy sessions. In trying to meet your child's many day-to-day needs, you may not have thought much about the variations in the role that temperament plays.

The outward expression of a child's temperament may be affected by her condition. If your child is not very verbal, for example, it may be less apparent whether she is outgoing in approach or withdrawing. If she is not able to walk, the activity trait may be moot. If she has a hearing impairment, traits such as sensitivity and distractibility may not seem relevant when it comes to noises in her environment.

All children have unique styles of interacting with their environment and the people in it. You should still consider your child's temperament patterns:

> You can profile your child's temperament just as you would for a child without a disability, using the suggestions in Chapter One.

> You can consider how your child's temperament influences you, as you did in Chapter Two.

> You can adapt management techniques from Chapter Three that will help improve the fit between your child's temperament and your parenting approach.

In evaluating your child's temperament, you will need to be careful as you compare your observations of your child's behavioral style with what you would expect for the average child of the same age. A normal attention span for a four-year-old developmental age may seem rather brief when the child's chronological age is six and a half years. Or, if your six-year-old is functioning at the level of a three-year-old in speech, you may need to adapt your interpretations and expectations of her temperament to her developmental age.

You may have to be a bit more creative in adapting the management suggestions in Chapter Three to your child's particular condition. You will be able to succeed if you view your child as an individual who, like all children, was born with a temperament all her own.

You may also want to keep in mind that other people in your child's life may make two common mistakes: Either they misinterpret his temperament, such as his stubbornness or shyness, as part of his disability; or they do not recognize your child as having a temperament at all. Unfortunately, before they see the person, too many people still see a label. "The deaf girl." "The retarded boy." If other people do not see a person, they surely will not look for temperament; nor will they recognize it if they do see it.

If someone significant in your child's life is making these mistakes, do not hesitate to point this out. Try to redirect that person's understanding by explaining your child's temperament: "Billy may not be able to tell you this in so many words, but he is generally shy. He certainly will be hesitant about going into the movie theater because people stare at him when we push his wheelchair into the special space where seats have been removed." "It takes Sandy a little longer to adapt to new situations." "Juan's very persistent. He likes to repeat a task over and over until he gets it right. I hope you'll give him some extra time to do so."

It is also useful to discuss your child's temperament with pediatricians, medical specialists, therapists, and others who work with and care for him. They are usually highly trained in their particular specialty; however, many are not well informed about temperament differences. Share your own observations about your child's temperament with these professionals and ask them to consider how these particular traits can be used to promote your child's development. Ask how information about his temperament could be incorporated into a plan for the best management of his condition.

Children with developmental delays or disabilities must be seen as individuals. For parents, physicians, psychologists, teachers, friends, and family members, it is imperative to treat each child with respect and affection. It is also equally important to recognize her individual temperament differences as they affect her behavior and development. By accommodating these differences for the best possible fit, you can manage them more easily, enhance maximum development, and avoid or solve behavior problems.

CHAPTER SIX

Temperament and Physical Health

Tyrone and Tarik are close in both age and affection. The brothers have been inseparable since Tarik was born, just eighteen months after Tyrone. They attend the same preschool and play with the same group of neighborhood friends. In physical appearance, the brothers resemble each other so strongly that adults often comment about their striking similarity.

The boys share a bedroom, toys, food, drinking glasses, towels, and occasionally the same toothbrush. They also generously share each other's germs. Whenever one catches a cold, the other is soon sneezing and coughing.

Tyrone and Tarik both have frequent ear infections, but their behavioral reactions to this discomfort differ dramatically. When Tyrone gets an earache, he lets everyone know about his pain. He screams loudly and long, and his parents have difficulty comforting him. When his earaches began at twelve months of age, his vigorous complaining prompted his parents to get immediate medical help.

When Tarik gets an earache (usually when Tyrone does), he reacts in an entirely different manner. He complains very little. At times, his ear infections were only discovered because he trotted along to a doctor's appointment that was scheduled for Tyrone. After examining Tyrone's inflamed eardrums, an alert pediatrician looked into Tarik's ears as well, even though he had not mentioned having pain. The doctor found on *several visits that Tarik's ear drums were equally as red and infected as Tyrone's.*

After the doctor prescribes the same antibiotic for both brothers, Tyrone usually continues to complain longer and more intensely than Tarik does. This sometimes leads the doctor to switch Tyrone to a different antibiotic after a few days because he seems not to be responding to the first one. She has suggested that his parents consider an operation to insert tubes in Tyrone's ears to decrease the frequency of infections. Yet the same treatment has not been suggested for Tarik, although he has had the same number of ear infections as his brother.

Temperament is ever-present. It does not disappear when a child is ill or injured. Just as it affects behavior, development, and school progress, temperament also influences physical health.

Research has demonstrated two basic connections between temperament and physical health. First, temperament predisposes some children to certain physical conditions (colic and injuries, for example), making them more likely to occur. Second, the sensitivity and reactivity components of temperament influence management and the outcome of physical health problems, as the case of Tyrone and Tarik illustrates. Because of Tyrone's characteristics—intensity, high sensitivity, and somewhat negative mood—his parents and pediatrician paid much more attention to Tyrone's physical ailments than they did to those of his brother, who was less sensitive to pain in his ears, much less intense about expressing discomfort, and generally more positive in mood. Tyrone's temperament may lead him to more treatment and for longer periods, whereas Tarik's pushes the odds in the opposite direction.

The notion that temperament and health are intertwined is not new. The founding fathers of Western medical science, Hippocrates about 400 B.C. and Galen in the second century A.D., thought that a mixture of the four basic "humors" (blood, yellow bile, black bile, and phlegm) determined both an individual's physical health and temperament. Their theory lasted a long time but was tossed into the historical dustbin well over one hundred years ago. Research on temperament in the past thirty years now confirms that there is a relationship, but not quite the one the ancients suggested. The modern findings indicate that the temperament–body link is through the nervous system, and not through the body fluids.

The role of temperament in the frequency of certain physical problems has two aspects. First, certain characteristics such as irritability may evoke more, or different, environmental responses that bring about a physical problem. For example, an infant's irritability is likely to result in increased parental attention, which may vary from appropriate soothing to overfeeding to abuse. Second, the child's style of reacting to stimuli of any kind may also make him more vulnerable to physical problems. For example, his greater sensitivity may increase the probability of sleep disturbances.

The outcome of physical illnesses is also affected by the same factors, but a little differently. The quality and quantity of a child's reaction to an illness are to some extent a reflection of the child's temperament, as illustrated by the contrasting ways Tyrone and Tarik respond to ear infections. The expression of these varied symptoms then can bring about changes in the amount of parental and medical attention given to a child, just as the two brothers seemed to receive different quantities of care for the same illnesses.

All children have physical health concerns from infancy through adolescence—some more than others in frequency, duration, and severity. Whether the problem is a routine head cold, a recurring condition such as asthma, or a congenital problem such as cystic fibrosis, parents and professional caregivers need to understand the child's individual temperament in order to fashion the best treatment plan. This chapter defines the role that a child's temperament plays in the occurrence and outcomes of physical conditions. The final section of the chapter suggests what parents can do to sort out and manage temperament issues when a child is ill or injured.

HOW TEMPERAMENT AFFECTS THE OCCURRENCE OF PHYSICAL PROBLEMS

ACCIDENTS AND INJURIES

Certain temperament traits predispose a child to specific health problems. In several studies, children whose temperament characteristics are considered challenging have been found to have more accidents and injuries; that is, they had cuts requiring stitches during infancy and hospital visits for a wide variety of injuries during the first five years of life. Another study, a detailed 1992 investigation that was part of the Louisville Twin Study, found that boys who were more withdrawn in initial reaction, negative in mood, low in both attention span and adaptability, and irregular in their sleep routines had more injuries than did children with "easier" temperament traits. Girls with injuries were distinguishable only by lower attention and more negative mood than their peer group.

This is not to say that certain traits make a child automatically "accident prone" at all times or throughout childhood. Too many other factors concerning the care givers and the household come into play. It is a common but inaccurate assumption that the activity trait is the only determinant of injuries or accidents. Although the level of activity is important, many highly active youngsters breeze through childhood without a stitch or a broken bone. Research studies have found instead that the common thread predisposing children to injuries is any combination of traits (but especially inattentiveness and the "difficult" traits mentioned above) that put a child in conflict—or out of touch—with an environment in which injuries are very possible.

Watch two seven-year-olds riding bikes through their neighborhood. One chatters and gestures as he whizzes along the sidewalk. He waves to friends and does not pay attention to curbs or toys left on the walk. When he comes to a street corner, he is distracted by the shouts of children playing basketball in a nearby driveway. He does not use his brakes. He rolls into the street where a car screeches to a stop and barely avoids hitting him.

The other seven-year-old has a much more cautious and attentive temperament. He never forgets to wear his helmet. He is not easily distracted. He watches the sidewalk immediately ahead of him and concentrates on steering his bike along a safe pathway. When he comes to a corner, he brakes and looks both ways before pedaling across the street.

The presence of potential hazards and the status of the caregivers matter as well. In a home in which parents are exhausted or emotionally overwhelmed, less attention may be paid to a curious toddler whose active, outgoing nature puts her in danger of falling, being burned by touching a stove or turning on scalding water, and other common household hazards. And less effort may be put into removing hazards such as dangerous medicines, toxic cleaning materials, electric wires, and guns.

COLIC

Colic has no standard definition and is not well understood. Many parents—and pediatric textbooks—consider colic a mysterious on-again, off-again cycle of abdominal pain. According to these books, colic has no specific cause and no apparent or effective remedy. It is not a complete mystery, however, and can usually be managed successfully.

A colicky infant is best described as one who is otherwise healthy and well fed but who cries excessively. The term *excessively* has been defined here as a total of more than three hours a day for more than three days in any one week during the first three or four months of life. There is no proof that there is pain in the abdomen or that there is any different sound to the crying. Colic is probably the earliest result of a poor fit between a baby's inborn temperament and parents' handling of the child.

Parents often use a trial-and-error approach to soothe the infant and nothing works—not more feedings, diaper changes, burping, rocking, picking up, and putting back down in the crib. My research and that of others shows that the problem generally consists of a normal irritable or sensitive temperament coupled with inappropriate handling. The parents do not understand the baby's needs and have not yet learned to read the baby's signals or respond in a harmonious way to soothe him and reduce his stress.

When I profiled formerly colicky babies of about four months of age, my research revealed challenging temperament traits, particularly irritability, and high sensitivity. Another study assessed temperament beginning at two weeks of age (before the colicky crying began) and predicted both duration and frequency of later crying. Other ongoing studies are looking into temperament traits at the time the colic is occurring.

A baby's temperament can be involved in several ways in colic. Greater irritability may lead his parents to try harder and do anything and everything to calm him. Sensitivity would cause him to be more vulnerable to their inconsistent attempts. As a result of their disorganized, on-again, off-again management style, he cries even more, particularly if his temperament characteristics also include intensity and low soothability.

Although all the answers are not in, it appears that not all babies with challenging temperament characteristics develop colic, and not all colicky infants have these traits. The key to understanding which baby develops colic and which does not lies in how parents respond to and handle each infant. There is usually nothing abnormal about either the infant or the parent.

Inappropriate handling is common, particularly among first-time parents who are inexperienced and anxious. They may not know how much normal infants cry (two to three hours a day in the first two months)or the most effective ways to calm babies, in general, and theirs, in particular. They may not read and interpret their baby's needs correctly. For example, when a baby begins to cry just a half hour after he has finished nursing for twenty minutes, his mother may assume that he is still hungry. She offers him more milk; of course, he will not take it because he is not hungry. Better management comes with improved understanding, more accurate observations of the baby's needs, and handling that decreases stimulation and increases soothing.

SLEEP PROBLEMS

By three or four months of age, most babies establish sleep–wake cycles that have been shaped by several influences, especially their natural body (circadian) rhythms, the extent to which parents try to organize daily routines, and the child's temperament. The regularity–irregularity trait is defined in part by the child's tendency to wake and go to sleep with or without a predictable pattern. This aspect of temperament modifies the success of parents' efforts to regulate and maintain normal sleep habits.

The adaptability and regularity traits come into play when parents try to establish a daytime nap routine. If parents of irregular children do not make a determined effort to schedule routine naps, these children are likely to have fewer naps and, perhaps, be more tired and irritable through the rest of the day.

If a child is negative in mood and quite intense, and thus cries louder than most, as well as being irregular and low in adaptability, her parents may have a difficult time with night awakening. Sensitivity to noises, lights, and damp diapers also matters. If parents respond to every cry in the middle of the night, they will be encouraging more crying by their overattention. These children usually do not wake up any more often during the night than others, but once awake they cannot soothe themselves back to sleep without crying and waking their parents. Depending on their intensity and persistence, babies who experience night awakening may cry loudly and long until someone picks them up and changes whatever stimuli are disturbing them, or they may fall back to sleep on their own.

Bedtime struggles may be influenced by temperament. A very persistent and irregular child may persuade indulgent parents to postpone bedtime. We have all heard those woeful pleas: "I need to finish this game first." "Just one more story." "I want a glass of water." "Sing me another song."

Whatever the temperament characteristics and whatever the child's age, if parents respond in ways that result in sleep deprivation, the end result is an overtired child. Sleep deprivation impairs attention and learning. It causes a stress response that can make the child more tense, aroused, and emotional. And that stress inevitably affects the rest of the family in negative ways.

As yet, no research has been done to clarify a possible role that temperament may play in the sleep problems of older children, such as nightmares and night terrors. Theoretically, we would expect a greater influence on nightmares because they are more reflective of stressful experiences during the day.

ABDOMINAL PAINS

"I have a stomachache. I can't go to school." When parents hear that refrain, their first thought is usually, "Is he really sick, or is he trying to get out of going to school?" When parents fall for that line, let him stay home, and then discover that he is eating and playing normally within an hour after the bus has left, they may feel foolish, manipulated, and annoyed, both at themselves and him. On the other hand, when they stand firm, insist that he go to school because the pain is minor and will go away, and later get a call from the school nurse saying that he has a fever, parents may then feel guilty or irresponsible.

Although it seems as if it is a no-win situation, parents can learn to read the reality of stomachaches, particularly if they are recurring. Parents can do so by looking more closely at the pattern, current stressors, and their child's temperament. They then can factor them into the immediate situation and arrive at a conclusion.

Several studies are informative on this point. A study of nearly two thousand children in Finland found that children under five years of age who were examined at a hospital for recurrent abdominal pains had been evaluated previously by their mothers as considerably more intense and negative in mood than other children. The mothers did the temperament assessments when their children were between six and eight months old. Did these children have more pain, or did they just complain more and louder?

Another study of six-year-old children in England found that recurrent abdominal pain correlated with challenging temperament traits, particularly withdrawing in initial reaction in boys and irregularity in girls. In this study abdominal pain was defined as three or more episodes of "incapacitating" pain over not less than three months. The British investigators found that the children reported more stomach pains near the start of the school year when they were adapting to new teachers, routines, and classmates. The frequency of abdominal pains decreased as the school year progressed; however, the children's temperament traits persisted.

Recurring abdominal pains can be caused by many factors. If no physical disease is present, a parent should consider the possibility that their child's temperament is exaggerating the effects of stressful experiences.

RECURRENT HEADACHES

In children as well as adults, stress is associated with the onset of migraine and tension headaches. The role of temperament in either increasing or alleviating that stress has received little attention. One small study of primary school children in Australia found that children who complained of headaches did not have a larger number of external stressors than other children; however, these children with headaches did exhibit some differences in behavioral style. They tended to be more shy and more sensitive than were other children in the study.

As with recurring abdominal pains, parents should consider, together with their child's doctor, that their child's temperament may be a contributor along with the other factors that are usually observed when a child complains of recurring headaches.

FEEDING AND GROWTH PROBLEMS

When investigators study feeding and growth problems as they relate to temperament, they tend to look into the more extreme cases, for example, obese youngsters, babies who fail to thrive, and children who survive famine. The following sections contain a summary of various findings that contribute to our overall understanding of the interaction between temperament and feeding problems and growth.

Obesity

Obesity is an increasingly common problem among American children. Nationwide studies now indicate that one in five children is obese. Obesity refers to weight in the ninety-fifth percentile or above for height, age, and gender. It results from taking in more calories than are expended, but is more complex than that. Why does one child seem to burn fewer calories than her brother or sister at the same activity level?

Once again, temperament contributes some answers. In one study of two hundred infants, I asked mothers to rate the temperaments of their babies, who ranged in age from six to twelve months. Of these infants, those whose mothers found them to have challenging temperaments, especially babies with negative moods, gained more weight for their heights than did other babies in the survey. I concluded that the fussier infants were fed more often in an attempt to soothe them.

In another study of children eight to twelve years of age, my colleagues and I found a relationship between temperament and obesity in a group of twenty-one of these children. The overweight children were less predictable and less persistent than those of normal weight.

What this means, and whether other investigators will uncover similar relationships, remains to be seen. For now, just remember that some children may have behavioral styles that put them at a risk for obesity.

Failure to thrive

The term *nonorganic failure to thrive* describes infants and toddlers who do not grow at the expected rate for age and gender and whose weight is abnormally low (below the fifth percentile) but have no physical disease to explain the growth problem. Although many factors may contribute to their low weight and slow growth, the general conclusion is that these babies do not receive an adequate intake of nutrition because there is a poor fit in the parent–child interaction. The parent does not feed the baby enough for one of several reasons. She may not "read" the baby's hunger cues correctly, or she may read the cues but not respond appropriately. Or the infant may not capture the parent's attention, and therefore, the parent does not recognize the child's real needs.

Several factors can add to the problem: The parent may be depressed or have other personal problems; unfavorable living conditions may divert the parent's attention and energy; an inexperienced parent may not know what nutritional requirements are needed by a young child.

Research also shows that children with certain temperament traits may not arouse the parent's attention or motivate the parent to provide adequate feeding. A quiet baby with low intensity, for example, does not cry very loudly to let her parents know how hungry she is. On the other hand, negative mood and other traits considered in the "difficult" cluster can turn off the parent before the child is properly fed. The child is fussy, does not smile, is demanding (that is, intense), and does not make the feeding interaction a pleasant, or even tolerable, experience. The stressed parent of a baby with this temperament is likely to cut short the feeding time or feed the baby less frequently. One result of this poor fit is an undernourished child who does not grow properly.

Survival of famine

Children who survive famine in parts of the world where severe drought and starvation cause thousands of deaths offer a dramatic finding that tells us more about temperament. In one study, a group of East African infants who were previously identified as having "easy" temperament traits were found to be more vulnerable to famine than were infants who did not have these traits. These amiable, uncomplaining babies had a much lower survival rate than did children whose temperaments were more challenging, that is, irritable and intense. It appears evident that in such severe conditions there is value in having challenging temperament traits. These children were apparently fed more of whatever meager food was available than were children with milder temperaments. A tentative conclusion may be d   from this example, as well as from failure-to-thrive studies: Children who complain little can be at risk of being underfed even in relatively more ordinary circumstances.

Tooth decay

Dental decay of the upper incisors in toddlers has received increasing attention since the 1970s. This problem was termed *bottle-mouth caries* because its cause was discovered to be prolonged bottle feedings during the day or night. Juice and milk are in such constant contact with the child's teeth that decay appears during infancy and the toddler years.

Early investigation pointed to several contributing factors: single-parent households, sleep difficulties, and the "strong temper" of the child. In many homes, a baby who is irritable, persistent, and difficult to soothe or distract is likely to be given a bottle to quiet him. Parents offer a fussy child a bottle of juice or milk at night. And it works. The baby quiets down, falls asleep, and sucks on the bottle off and on during the night. The practice becomes as much a part of the bedtime routine as pajamas and night-lights.

The ever-present bottle, however, can be replaced with other soothing substitutes: a bottle of water instead of juice or milk, or a pacifier. The parent can then gradually wean the child from anything inserted in the mouth to rocking, lullabies, or stuffed animals.

BOWEL AND BLADDER FUNCTION

We are not aware of any formal studies concerning the relationship of temperament to toilet training, but surely there is one. Chapter Five discusses how much temperament is involved in the maturation of function.

Encopresis

After four years of age, some children regularly soil their clothing because they retain feces, and leakage results. This is called *encopresis*. It is a distressing problem for both children and parents, and one that is incompletely understood. A generation ago, encopresis was believed to be a sign of a severe emotional disturbance because no physical cause could be found and brief counseling did not correct the problem. During the 1970s, however, studies failed to prove any severe emotional cause in most cases.

Currently, some researchers believe (based on unproved clinical impressions) that children with this condition may not have a greater number of behavioral disorders but may have more temperamental "difficulty" than children without encopresis. Low adaptability may contribute to their resistance or reluctance to use the bathroom and to adjust to new or unfamiliar suggestions from their parents or doctor.

Enuresis

In the past, bed-wetting, or *enuresis*, also has been blamed on emotional problems. However, it is now believed that bed-wetting has several possible physiological causes. Because it occurs when the child is asleep, the cause seems unlikely to involve a temperament–environment interaction. However, the child's response to management efforts may be affected by his temperament.

EFFECTS OF TEMPERAMENT ON OUTCOME OF ILLNESS

REACTION TO ILLNESS

As the story of Tyrone and Tarik has demonstrated, the outcome of an illness can be influenced by a child's individual temperament. The less complaining child, like Tarik, may not receive early and prompt attention. Medical care may be insufficient for children like Tarik because his temperament does not draw as much attention to his physical discomfort as does that of a complaining child. The traits of low sensitivity to pain, low intensity about expressing pain, a positive mood, greater adaptability, a tendency to be easily distracted from the discomfort, alone or in combination with others, can result in fewer complains from the child about a physical problem. Children with these traits are much easier for parents to care for when they are sick or injured. They also are more likely to cooperate with whatever treatment is called for, even though it may be painful or otherwise unpleasant.

Children with temperament traits at the opposite pole, such as high sensitivity and intensity, are far more likely to voice their distress sooner and more emphatically than are those with easy traits. Their distress will probably bring about a more rapid response from parents, doctors, nurses, and child care workers; however, these children are in some danger of getting too much attention. Although few formal studies have been done, experience tells us that this probably applies to most of the common illnesses of childhood.

USE OF MEDICAL SERVICES

Several research studies show that temperament also affects how frequently medical services are sought. In my own pediatric practice, I reviewed several hundred infants, some of whom had been identified as having the more challenging temperament traits. In their first two years of life, their parents brought them in for more visits for various illnesses and injuries than did parents of babies with easy temperaments. Although one could not rule out the possibility that they may have had more medical problems, children with more challenging temperaments clearly provoke more anxiety in their parents (and physician) because they complain more.

Another survey elsewhere looked at children aged 6 to 9 years who were enrolled in a health maintenance organization. Those youngsters who were found to be more negative in mood or lower in distractibility than other children made considerably more visits to the doctor.

For children with some chronic conditions, temperament seems to play a significant role in their staying with the treatment plan. Youngsters with diabetes mellitus, whose blood sugar must be monitored closely, have been studied for temperament as it relates to compliance with specific medical management plans. Those children with high attention span demonstrated both better blood-sugar control and adherence to prescribed regimens.

RESPONSE TO HOSPITALIZATION

When children need hospitalization or surgery, the prospect of separation from parents and admission to an unfamiliar hospital setting is frightening for any child. Physical pain and discomfort only add to that normal anxiety. Prior hospital experiences may or may not prove helpful, and even the most adaptable child is challenged. Temperament plays an influential role in children's reaction to this experience.

Several studies have looked at this connection between temperament and response to hospitalization. In one study, children four to twelve years of age who were admitted for tonsillectomies had previously been evaluated for temperament traits. Their high regularity, approaching manner in initial reactions, adaptability, and positive mood predicted their smoother adjustment to hospitalization quite clearly.

In another sample of children who had genitourinary surgery (mostly to correct undescended testicles), those previously rated higher in intensity were given more medication by nurses on an "as needed" standing medication order. The conclusion was that the more forcefully these children complained, the more they were seen as suffering and in need of medication.

If temperament traits could be bought off the shelf, most parents would purchase a supply of adaptability, persistence, and positive mood when they pack their child's things for a hospital stay. These characteristics clearly help the child who undergoes extensive or unfamiliar procedures by making it easier for him to accept and stick to prescribed plans, as unpleasant as they may be.

Whether or not a child is endowed with these traits, parents, physicians, and hospital staff all can contribute to aiding the child during this difficult time. Preparation for what will happen and what to expect can help your child's behavioral and emotional response. Nurturing support during the experience also is essential. Some children will need more assistance than others do, depending in part on their temperaments.

If you know that your child is particularly sensitive to pain, adapts to strange situations slowly and apprehensively, or is particularly intense, do tell the doctor and hospital staff who come in contact with your child. They then will be able to incorporate this understanding into an overall treatment plan tailored to your child's emotional and physical needs.

HOW TO USE THIS INFORMATION TO IMPROVE YOUR CHILD'S HEALTH

Now that you have profiled your child's individual temperament, you understand how it influences behavior and development. With that knowledge you have probably already started to respond differently to your child in ways that can better the fit between temperament and environment. You may already be seeing improvement in his behavior as a result, and it is our hope that you are experiencing less stress within the family's interaction.

You can now begin to apply your understanding of temperament to health care, both to your child's vulnerabilities to common childhood illness and injuries and to reactions to illnesses. Does your child have an "illness style," a distinctive set of behaviors when sick? Begin by going back to the notebook of temperament observations you compiled for Chapter One. Were any of those observations made at a time when your child was injured or not feeling well, for example, when she was coming down with a cold or recovering from a sprained ankle?

Review your observations with an eye to physical health and how it was influenced by your child's particular temperament. If your earlier temperament observations were made during a time when your child had no health problems, that is fortunate for him. But you may want to pull out your notebook the next time he has some physical symptoms or complaints and add some further observations.

An understanding of the role that temperament plays in physical health can help clarify how serious his complaint really is. Obviously, if you have any doubt about a child's symptoms or expressions of discomfort, the wisest course is to ask his doctor. Even the best understanding of temperament is not a diagnosis of a physical condition. However, it can shed light on the situation.

Try to estimate the degree to which temperament may have influenced the cause of a particular health problem or your child's reaction to it. Look for patterns that may reveal the connections between his temperament and occasions when he became ill or injured. Let's say, for example, that you have determined your son to be quite active, with a low attention span. How does he react when you remind him to wear his helmet when riding his bike or rollerblading? Does he comply with a smile or a scowl? Does he protest or object, or even ignore you, once he goes outside? Does he seem to fall more and get more injuries than his friends do? Does he cry loudly, or does he silently tear up when he scrapes his elbow?

When the doctor tells your daughter that she cannot return to gymnastics lessons until her stress fracture has healed, how does she respond—with or without much protest or complaint? When she had the chicken pox, did she follow your advice about not scratching? How often does she complain of abdominal pains or headaches, and do those complaints follow any pattern? Do they seem more frequent on Sunday nights or Monday mornings at the beginning of a new school week? Are they most likely to arise when she is stressed or after she has eaten particular foods?

As your children grow older, you can share your insights with them and help them to become better able to manage their own health.

If environmental stressors are contributing to a physical problem, try to reduce their influence. Try decreasing the household noise for the sensitive child with night awakening, or eliminating unnecessary annoyances in the life of a child experiencing recurring headaches.

The management of overfeeding, colic, and the common sleep problems consists largely of learning to read your child's real needs and meeting them without being misled by the "noise" (or possibly misleading influence) of the temperament. For example, your child's volume of crying is not necessarily an accurate measure of his degree of hunger or amount of discomfort. With abdominal pain and headaches, remember that the reports of discomfort may be more a reflection of the child's style of reacting to stress than a reliable indicator of the magnitude of the stress.

When children are sick or injured, modifying medical or nursing care to accommodate their temperaments may also be helpful. If the attending doctors and nurses do not know your child or do not pay attention to his temperament, explain from your experience how his particular style may affect his health and treatment. Any such measures will only help recovery and improve health care.

Before Tyrone checked into the hospital to have tubes inserted into his ears, his parents tried to prepare him in ways that would help ease his fears. Recognizing his temperament as very intense, sensitive, and low in adaptability, they explained what would happen when he went to the hospital, and they initiated role-playing games, with Tyrone taking turns as both patient and doctor. His parents also telephoned the hospital to ask if they could bring their son by in advance to show him around. They happily discovered that this hospital offered a mini-tour for children that included a cartoon-style video used to prepare youngsters for hospitalization.

Let's not forget brother Tarik, the rare complainer. Once his parents understood the role that temperament plays in physical health, they talked to Tarik about "what hurts." They walked a fine line between over- and underemphasis of physical symptoms. They told him that he should tell his mother or father whenever he got hurt or did not feel quite right. Tarik's parents did not project excessive concern about every little scratch or bump; however, they did send a clear message that it is okay to express physical discomfort. They also kept a sharper eye on him when they thought he had been exposed to an infection or was not quite himself. They had learned that his low-key temperament did not naturally prompt him to complain about physical symptoms.

CHAPTER SEVEN

Temperament in Day Care and School

W hether your child is currently in day care or in nursery, elementary, or secondary school, her individual temperament strongly affects how she fares socially and academically. During the day care and preschool years, temperament has an important impact on development and behavior. As children move into grade school and continue through high school, the focus shifts toward the contribution temperament makes to academic achievement. Although most of this chapter concerns the influence of temperament on school performance, let's start at the beginning, with the day care and nursery school years, because today, most American children enter some sort of formal, organized program outside the home at an early age.

PRESCHOOL CHILD CARE AND EDUCATION

When children are still infants and toddlers, a clear understanding of temperament helps their parents get them off to a good start in the areas of development, behavior, and health. During these early years, parents are the primary promoters of the good fit that they hope to achieve between their child's individual temperament and her environment.

Children do not stay home very long. Whether you enroll your child in day care at six months of age, nursery school at three years, or kindergarten at five, you hand off some major responsibility to other adults. You may become quickly aware that these caregivers have different ideas than you have about your child, and their management styles may vary from yours as well.

Many of these caregivers will be very experienced with young children. Some of them will take your child's unique temperament into consideration and try, as you do, to promote a good fit. Others will be less experienced or inadequately trained. They may know little about temperament, in general, and even less about your own child's. The studies of temperament in day care are scanty but sufficient to indicate that it is as important there as at home.

> *We met Suzannah in the Introduction. She has always been a "spirited" child, as her parents aptly describe her; she can be irritable and explosive if she does not get her way. At home they handle her skillfully by praising and encouraging her sunny side, while standing firm about unacceptable behaviors, such as her temper tantrums. When she was about to begin day care at age 3, they worried that she might have some difficulty fitting in.*
>
> *Her parents were happily surprised during the first few weeks of day care. Notes from the teacher were sent home in Suzannah's lunch box: "She is such a little ray of sunshine." "Suzannah is getting along well with the other children." Apparently this new day care adventure was exciting and pleasant for her, they concluded. Her outgoing nature seemed to thrive in her new day care world.*
>
> *One evening, the teacher phoned unexpectedly to report that Suzannah had tossed a tantrum and pushed another child that day. Suzannah's teacher was surprised at this outburst and asked her parents to come in for a conference. Fortunately, Suzannah's teacher was experienced and calm. She and Suzannah's parents sat down to discuss both the incident and Suzannah's temperament. Together they agreed that she was a spirited, normal child who just needed some help*

handling her temper. They also shared information about her appealing characteristics—her zest, positive mood, and sense of humor—that they could build on to help her adapt better when a situation did not go exactly to her liking. For the next two years of day care, Suzannah adjusted satisfactorily.

Moving into the larger universe outside the home is challenging for most children. For the first time in their short lives, they are expected to get along with large numbers of other youngsters. New adults are in charge. Regulations and routines are unfamiliar. Foods, sights, sounds, and the rhythms of the day suddenly have changed. Hanging up a jacket, finding the bathroom, and even discovering when they may use the bathroom are small details that adults take for granted. All are novel experiences for a child first entering a day care center or preschool.

As we have seen with other dimensions of a child's life, some temperament traits can help smooth his entrance into this wider world. Traits such as positive mood, an approaching manner in initial reactions, and high adaptability are assets when a child begins a structured program. Other traits may be plusses or minuses, depending largely on the program itself. A highly regular child, for example, has been accustomed to eating and napping at the same times every day at home. When he enters a day care center with a very loosely organized schedule, he may have difficulty adjusting. If he were in a day care center that provided a more structured program, however, there would be no problem. Similarly, an active child will thrive in a setting in which running, jumping, and other physical activities are encouraged. That same child would probably chafe in a program in which these opportunities are limited.

When parents look for day care programs and nursery schools, their initial concerns are usually about whether the school is affordable and convenient. Then, when they visit the site, their eyes are drawn first to the physical surroundings. They ask themselves some questions. Is the play area roomy, safe, and attractive? Is the nap area quiet and set apart from the children who are not napping? Is the whole place cheerfully decorated? Is it clean? Are the toys stimulating?

When shopping for the most appropriate preschool program for your child, you will probably ask yourself these questions in a new light, now that you know about the role that temperament plays in your child's life. If your youngster is sensitive to noises and easily distracted, a day care center or nursery school without a quiet nap area will not be appropriate. Other children may be able to fall asleep in the middle of a room where others are talking and walking about, but not yours.

You will also look at the other children. Are there many children in a single room? Do they look happy? Are they engaged in activities that seem to captivate and hold their attention? How do they get along with each other? How physically active are they? Do they move about freely, or are they confined to limited areas? If you are wondering what these questions have to do with temperament, try to envision your child in this group. Now that you understand her temperament, do you think she can achieve a good fit with this particular group of children?

The most important observations you will make when visiting a day care or nursery program concern the staff. Are there enough adults to supervise the number of children? Do the adults treat each child as an individual, or do they seem to expect all the children to behave or participate in a uniform way? How do they manage youngsters who are having a conflict about sharing a toy? How do they handle that shy child on the fringe of the group? How do they manage the loud, highly active child who is disrupting other children's activities?

An understanding, well-trained staff is the hope of every parent who enrolls a young child in a day care center or nursery school. Most of the time, those hopes are fulfilled, but some staff members may not meet your expectations. Many are overworked and underpaid. If you believe that your child is not well understood or well cared for, do not hesitate to request a conference with the center's director and the classroom teacher.

Ask about their observations of your child. If they use vague labels such as "bossy," "immature," or "hyper" to describe her, ask for more specific examples of her behavioral style in actual situations. Explain what you have learned about your child's individual temperament. Describe the management techniques that work best at home. Discuss which approaches the teacher can use in the classroom and you can use at home to ensure consistency in the child's management.

Many times, teachers and day care workers may be more objective than parents are. Do not be surprised if their observations of your child's behavioral style are different from yours. This does not mean the teacher is incorrect. Besides, a child does not necessarily react or behave the same way in all settings. The point is to share your observations of temperament and reach an agreement on what works best for your child.

Recall from the Introduction how Michael's parents helped ease his adjustment to day care by discussing his shy temperament with his teacher, who had originally labeled him "emotionally insecure." After his parents explained that his reticence in new situations was part of Michael's normal nature and that he warmed up if given a little extra time and gentle encouragement, the teacher was able to apply this new understanding successfully to her dealings with Michael.

Too often, children acquire labels in day care or nursery school that stick with them through their years of formal schooling. They may be called "stubborn," "wild," "supersensitive," "a loudmouth," or worse. Some temperament traits may support these labels to an extent; however, such descriptions should be strongly discouraged even if they hold a fraction of truth, because they will affect the attitudes of the adults who will care for your child. And sometimes your child's peers pick up on these labels and use them.

If such labels are passed on, they may predispose a future teacher in grade school to expect certain behaviors even before the child has had a chance to settle into the class. Some studies have shown that teachers tend to alter their management of a student because of their expectations for performance. If a teacher expects a particular child to be persistent and highly adaptable and to have a high attention span and a pleasant mood, that child probably will get more of the teacher's positive attention than would another child who has a reputation for low persistence, intensity, inflexibility, and negative mood. Several studies have demonstrated how a child's temperament influences teachers' attitudes, which in turn affect the child's behavior and school performance.

When discussing your child's temperament traits with teachers and other caregivers, be sure that the temperament profile is accurate and well understood and that it is not used to label him in a judgmental way.

SCHOOL PERFORMANCE AND ADJUSTMENT

Parents usually have some choice when selecting a day care center or preschool. As their children reach school age, parents have fewer options about classes, programs, and teachers. Whether parents send their children to a public, private, or religious-affiliated school, wide variation among the staff can exist within a single school.

A child may fall in love with her first-grade teacher and have a wonderful school year. The next year, that same child may not get along nearly as well with another teacher whose style may be quite different. Throughout any child's school career, circumstances and players change frequently. For that reason, parents are cautioned to keep temperament in mind not only when a child enters school, but also whenever teacher conferences are held and whenever a child has a problem with a teacher or the classroom environment.

To understand better the role that temperament plays in school performance, let's first look at two children, Darren and Susan. Although they share a similar temperament, each one's school performance was affected by their temperament to a different degree.

When Darren was halfway through first grade, his teacher reported that although he seemed to be quite bright, he could not sit still and pay attention to lessons. Both she and his parents agreed that Darren's performance was inadequate and his self-esteem seemed low. They feared that his early school behaviors might lead to long-term academic failure if something were not done to turn it around quickly. The teacher suggested that his parents ask their pediatrician about medication for Darren.

Darren's pediatrician had cared for him since he was a toddler and knew that Darren had neither a physical nor a neurological problem. The doctor discussed temperament with Darren's parents and, using a standardized temperament questionnaire, asked them questions about Darren's behavioral style. Both the test results and the parents' own observations agreed that Darren displayed low persistence and attention span, high distractibility, and high activity. The doctor explained that, when clustered together, these traits are often referred to as "low task orientation" or "slow work style," which is another way to describe the inattention and restlessness reported by Darren's teacher.

The doctor asked if the school had given Darren psychological tests. When the doctor learned that testing had not been done and would not be done for several months, he arranged for a psychologist to examine Darren. The psychological testing revealed that Darren had high intelligence but some information-processing disabilities in the areas of visual-motor skills and spatial perception.

Together, the pediatrician, teacher, psychologist, and parents worked out a plan to help Darren. This plan included both medication (methylphenidate, commonly known as Ritalin) and changes in handling his behavior at home and in school. Darren's schoolwork, self-esteem, and family interactions soon improved. His temperament did not change; however, his school performance and personal adjustment became much better. Darren was treated with methylphenidate for two years. After that time, the drug treatment was withdrawn. Darren is now doing average work in high school with tutorial help.

Susan was equally bright but had only a mediocre school record. Out of curiosity, her mother profiled Susan's temperament at six years of age and then again at ten years. At both ages, Susan displayed characteristics that amounted to low task orientation or slow work style, just as Darren had. Psychological testing revealed no learning disabilities, and neither her parents and teachers saw any behavioral or emotional problems.

Susan was fortunate to have supportive parents and experienced, understanding teachers. Throughout twelve years of school, she scored high on aptitude tests but had only average scores on achievement tests. Given her intellectual abilities, she would have to have been considered an underachiever because she earned mostly B's and a few C's, despite aptitude tests indicating she could have earned A's.

During high school, Susan typically put off writing term papers and studying for tests until the last minute. Her high intelligence and ability to work quickly under pressure always pulled her through. Her parents were not thrilled with her study habits and were mildly disappointed in her average grades; however, they did not worry. Her school counselor was somewhat dissatisfied with her academic work but did not suggest referral for medication or special testing. Early in her senior year of high school, the counselor and her parents were concerned that her poor study habits could lead to failure in the less structured environment of college. They held their collective breaths when she went off to college.

Susan's story had a happy ending. In college, her intelligence and newly activated intellectual curiosity overcame her old study habits and carried her through to graduate with high honors.

Darren and Susan had similar temperaments, IQs, families, and schools. In both cases, their temperaments affected their academic achievement. Darren's problems were greater because of his learning disability. He had a difference in brain function, which created greater academic obstacles, and more need for external help. With no learning disability, Susan changed from an underachiever to a good academic performer when her own internal motivation helped her to overcome poor work habits.

Like Susan, Andy (from the Introduction) had temperament traits that aroused some comment and concern at school and at home. But because both Susan and Andy were doing well enough, no intervention was suggested. Andy was just regarded as "a scatterbrained kid" or "the absent-minded professor."

IMPACT OF TEMPERAMENT ON ACADEMIC PERFORMANCE

As Darren and Susan illustrate, temperament contributes to "task orientation," or a child's style of handling such things as following instructions, doing classroom chores, listening to the teacher and other students, completing assignments within an allotted time, and paying attention to a new lesson or slide presentation.

With the growing number of children experiencing preschool in the form of day care or nursery programs, many youngsters are introduced to the need for task orientation well before first grade. They are expected to name colors, letters, and animals, and to count numbers. They become acclimated to an organized community, and they learn to conform to rules and regulations, for example, finishing their snacks in time to go outdoors with the other children and putting their puzzles, games, and books back on the shelf when they have completed an activity.

In middle childhood, between the ages of 6 and 12 years, more demanding academic requirements call for greater attention, persistence, and adaptability. Children at this stage of life now live in a complex world of standardized education in which social and behavioral adjustments continue to be important, but where cognitive development takes greater prominence. Although the academic challenges are new, the child's innate temperament is not new. It has been part of her since early infancy. In kindergarten or first grade, the child and her temperament characteristics are introduced to an unfamiliar environment. Teachers now expect her to pay attention, sit still, and avoid distractions, requirements that were far less demanding in day care or preschool.

As early as the 1960s, psychiatrists Alexander Thomas and Stella Chess and their fellow investigators in the New York Longitudinal Study began to explore the effect of temperament on teachers' attitudes toward students and on students' performance on achievement tests. Since the 1980s, several psychologists have also begun to evaluate the impact of temperament on accomplishment of schoolwork. The most important information has come from Dr. Barbara Keogh and her associates at the University of California, Los Angeles, and Dr. Roy Martin and his colleagues at the University of Georgia, Athens, Georgia. (See Resources at the end of this book.) They have demonstrated that temperament has a major impact *directly* on how efficiently a student works and *indirectly* affects academic performance by way of its influence on teachers' attitudes toward the student.

Their most significant finding is that several temperament traits, especially persistence and attention span, whether rated by parents or teachers, are related both to grades and to scores on standardized achievement tests, regardless of the child's intelligence level. (And none of children studied had been diagnosed with an attention deficit hyperactivity disorder.) More attention and persistence mean better performance. The same is true for low distractibility and low activity. In fact, a child's temperament seems to contribute more to results than does his IQ. Apparently, these behavioral style traits increase or decrease his efficiency at learning new material, in using what he already knows, and perhaps also in test-taking skills. Teachers' ratings of high attention span and persistence, low distractibility, and low activity, for example, were shown to be related to better performance on standardized achievement tests in reading and mathematics in the elementary school grades up to five years later, regardless of the child's intelligence level.

These conclusions appear to apply to children at all levels of cognitive or learning ability and over a wide range of socioeconomic circumstances. The outcome depends on various aspects of the fit between the temperament, age, cognitive skills, and motivation of the child, the subject matter, and teachers' attitudes and styles.

The relationship between temperament and intelligence or learning abilities is debated by the researchers. Certainly, temperament does strongly affect the efficiency with which a person uses his or her learning abilities.

The other most significant finding is the way children's temperament influences how their teachers view them. One study of kindergarten children showed that their teachers tended to overestimate the intelligence of children who were approaching in their initial reactions and more adaptable. Their behavioral style evidently made them seem brighter.

Other studies have demonstrated that teachers prefer children who are less active, less distractible, and more persistent and attentive. We may assume that these preferences express themselves in the way a teacher actually handles classroom management and designs instructional strategies.

ADOLESCENTS

Studies of temperament in adolescence are few, but available information gives us good reason to believe that temperament continues to influence academic performance during the teen years. After all, the definition and dimensions of temperament have not changed. Genetic and other contributions remain about the same as they were earlier in childhood, although new physical factors may now play a role: increased levels of the sex hormones, dietary changes, sleep deprivation, rigorous athletic training, and drug and alcohol abuse. A significant positive adaptation is that teenagers are more likely than are younger children to have developed the ability to alter the expression of reaction style patterns consciously and voluntarily. For example, they have frequently worked out strategies for forcing themselves to pay attention when it really matters and to minimize the disruptions caused by their distractibility.

In fact, many of the studies purporting to investigate attention deficit/hyperactivity disorder (ADHD) in adolescence are probably detecting normal temperament traits. More on this complex issue later in this chapter.

SCHOOL BEHAVIORAL PROBLEMS

When a child enters school for the very first time or enrolls in a new school later on, several temperament traits come into play in adjusting to the new social situation. If he is slow to warm up and does not adapt to unfamiliar situations easily, he may withdraw or hold back and not settle in smoothly. Teachers may consider him anxious, insecure, or immature. This was true of Michael in the Introduction, and it can happen with older children as well. Characteristics such as low persistence, high distractibility, high activity, shyness, low adaptability, and negative mood can contribute to classroom behaviors—social as well as academic—that teachers and classmates find troublesome, just as parents do.

A child with some or all of these traits may be managed well at home by understanding parents; however, this combination can result in a poor fit at school if the teacher's knowledge and handling of the child differs from his parents' values, expectations, and style. On the other hand, the fit is sometimes better at school than at home. Conferences with the teacher should be helpful in improving the problem with fit. What works at home and what works at school may be the same or different.

THE ATTENTION DEFICIT/ HYPERACTIVITY DISORDER CONFUSION

The definition, diagnosis, and management of ADHD is a baffling and highly emotional topic, as well as a source of great confusion among parents, educators, psychologists, physicians, and the general public. In this section, the extent of the epidemic is reviewed: where it came from, what went wrong, the problems with the present diagnostic system, and what can be done until the situation is clarified.

THE EPIDEMIC

Some children indeed have learning disabilities and neurological problems that limit their ability to pay attention and that impair their achievement in school. But the fact that up to 10 percent of the children in this country are being diagnosed with ADHD is unrealistically out of proportion with what we know about temperament and neurological science.

The numbers are staggering. In 1995, more than 1.3 million children—out of 38 million American children between the ages of 5 and 14 years—were estimated to be taking Ritalin, a brain-stimulating drug, for treatment of ADHD. Some reports, which do not account for age ranges, have placed the total number as high as 2 million children.

The October 1995 background paper on methylphenidate by the Drug Enforcement Administration (DEA) reported:

> *Since 1990, there has been a six-fold increase in the U.S. production and utilization of methylphenidate. This increase contrasts sharply with trends in medical practice seen in the rest of the world . . . . the U.S. produces and consumes five times more methylphenidate than the rest of the world combined.*

Ritalin is big business. In 1995, sales of the medication, which has been classified as a controlled substance by the DEA since 1971, were reported to be over $350 million. Ritalin is the most widely used drug for ADHD. Dexedrine (dextroamphetamine) and Cylert (pemoline) are prescribed less often.

In the past few years, ADHD and Ritalin have received such broad media attention that parents themselves "diagnose" ADHD and teachers have come to suggest that children be taken to a doctor to obtain a prescription for Ritalin. It is not uncommon today to hear one parent suggest to another that her very active, impulsive, fidgety four-year-old "is ADHD" and would benefit from Ritalin. School psychologists report that anxious parents sometimes pressure them to recommend medication before their child is even evaluated.

When pediatricians were surveyed for a report in one of the leading pediatric journals, nearly half of them reported that they frequently prescribe Ritalin after an examination lasting only a few minutes and without consulting teachers, reviewing educational levels, or seeking a psychological workup. The survey also found that most medical doctors rarely recommend anything other than these pills, such as behavioral therapy or special help in school. The 1995 background paper by the DEA also stated:

> *Epidemiological data indicate that from 3 to 5 percent or more of all U.S. children are treated with methylphenidate for ADHD, frequently without the benefit of other services as recommended in treatment guidelines.*

This is inadequate medical care.

ORIGIN OF THE DIAGNOSIS

The origins of the ADHD concept can be traced back to the 1920s when it was thought that brain-injured children shared characteristic behaviors. In the 1960s, the United States Public Health Service tried to clarify these behaviors and offered a definition of "minimal brain dysfunction," as opposed to "minimal brain damage." In 1968, the American Psychiatric Association (APA), in its *Diagnostic and Statistical Manual of Mental Disorders, Second Edition* (DSM-II), described it under the new label of "hyperkinetic reaction of childhood" with words such as "overactivity, restlessness, distractibility, and short attention span"; however, these characteristics were not delineated and no criteria were given for diagnosis.

In subsequent DSM editions (III in 1980 and III-R in 1987), the APA changed the name to attention deficit disorder and then to attention deficit/hyperactivity disorder and offered fourteen behavioral descriptions, eight of which must be present for at least six months for a diagnosis to be confirmed. The most recent edition of the DSM, DSM-IV, published in 1994, refines ADHD still further to make the diagnosis dependent on the presence of either six out of nine inattention criteria or six out of nine hyperactivity/impulsivity criteria. However, the qualifying descriptions of behavior continue to be quite general and vague, such as "often has difficulty organizing tasks and activities," "often talks excessively," or "often has difficulty playing or engaging in leisure activities quietly."

The latest DSM-IV does takes a step forward by including two new requirements: "There must be clear evidence of clinically significant impairment in social, academic, or occupational functioning," and this impairment must be present in two or more settings, such as school, work, or home.

The DSM-IV still falls short, however, by perpetuating unclear standards for defining the behaviors. It says, for example, that behaviors are "more frequent and severe than is typically observed in individuals at a comparable level of development." Such a description could be applied to most of us; that is, anyone could qualify if he were above average in activity or below average in attentiveness.

WHAT WENT WRONG?

Several social and historical factors have contributed to this confusing epidemic. The principal one for discussion in this book, and probably the most important of all, can be stated simply: In the last thirty years, the old view of blaming all of a child's behavior problems on parents—and especially mothers—has been discarded. Now the pendulum has swung to the opposite extreme of blaming too much on the child. Rapid acceptance of this shift by parents and schools is understandable.

With ADHD, the problem is commonly regarded as being all within the child and not at all related to interactions with the environment. Unfortunately, the developers of the ADHD concept have ignored the existence and importance of temperament. They have generally failed to recognize that almost all variations in activity and attention are *normal*, and that only in exceptional cases is there evidence of a definite problem with the child's brain. The outcome for the individual child depends mainly on the fit of his temperament traits with his environment at school and at home. This basic concept is missing in most works on ADHD.

PROBLEMS WITH THE ATTENTION DEFICIT/ HYPERACTIVITY DISORDER DIAGNOSIS

The outstanding deficiency in the ADHD diagnostic system, as it stands today, is that ADHD is an oversimplified grouping of a complex and variable set of normal but incompatible temperament variations, disabilities in learning, problems in school function and behavior, and sometimes neurological immaturity. A great variety of children's problems is being compressed into a single label: ADHD. Consequently, teachers, physicians, and psychologists frequently offer differing opinions about whether a specific child has the condition.

The ADHD diagnosis has failed to recognize that half of normal children are more active, more inattentive, or more distractible than average. No clear guidelines are offered about at which point normal leaves off and abnormal begins. What is the difference between high activity and "hyperactivity" or between normal inattentiveness and an abnormal "attention deficit"? Is it just a matter of degree? Or are there differences in the quality of the behavior? Furthermore, inattentiveness may be due to a wide range of other causes, including fatigue, a physical illness, a learning disability, anxiety, and depression.

Some who exhibit the component behaviors of what is now thought of as ADHD are doing satisfactorily or even quite well. How can that be? Clearly, some factors other than the predisposing inattentiveness and activity must be present. However, the ADHD diagnostic criteria do not ask for an evaluation of them. The stories of Susan and Andy illustrate how, when other attributes in a child and his environment are favorable, the inattentiveness and activity do not necessarily lead to a problem in school. For Susan and Andy, their other qualities and their supportive families and schools helped to compensate for their less task-oriented traits such as inattentiveness.

The most common problem for children who are now being diagnosed with ADHD may be a deficiency of self-regulation, as a leading researcher in the field, Dr. Russell Barkley of the University of Massachusetts, Medical Center, Worcester, Massachusetts, suggests, rather than inattentiveness or activity. In terms of temperament characteristics, that means that low adaptability may be the key trait, a point demonstrated by my group's research and reported almost twenty years ago. The combination of low adaptability and inattentiveness may be most likely to impair school performance and lead to the diagnosis of ADHD.

The term *impulsivity* is used as one of the criteria for the diagnosis of ADHD. It refers to the rate at which children translate thoughts and feelings into action. A highly impulsive child does so quickly and without hesitation, rather than taking his time to consider the outcome of his action.

Impulsivity is probably more a part of behavioral adjustment than a basic, inherited trait. It seems likely that a child's establishment of impulse control lies as much, or more, in the degree to which parents and other caregivers train the child to develop self-restraint. Therefore, if a child is considered as possibly having ADHD, it is important to look closely at whether adults are guiding the child toward more self-control and away from impulsivity, and if so, how.

Some physicians and psychologists have estimated that as many as 10 percent of children have ADHD. Yet there is no proof that so many children have brain abnormalities. It seems implausible that, after millennia of evolution, the human race has reached a point where 10 percent of its members could have defective brains. Less than one percent is what better research is likely to reveal.

WHAT TO DO

There is little justification for formal temperament measurements for the average or superior student who is progressing satisfactorily in school. The professional time required would be better used for less fortunate children. Nevertheless, informal teacher assessments are always appropriate. But if problems in school performance or behavior arise, consideration of the child's temperament could be very useful. Parents should be sure to share their understanding of their child's traits with the teacher or guidance counselor and make certain that the school's authorities recognize these traits. Counselors would be helped in their evaluations by a temperament scale appropriate for use in schools. (See Resources at the back of this book.)

If inattention has been identified as a problem, my views about the confusion over ADHD might seem unsettling. That is far from my intention: I do not want to add to the confusion; I want to help clarify it.

If a teacher, school psychologist, friend, neighbor, or relative tells you that your youngster is hyperactive or has ADHD, do not become alarmed. The ADHD label has become so widely applied that many people casually bandy it about in every forum, from talk shows to playgrounds. Clearly, it means different things to different people.

No precise diagnostic test exists for ADHD. A great deal of medical and psychological research is needed. Long-term studies are necessary to clarify which factors lead to the various clinical problems that are now lumped together under this label. Tests of brain function are needed to hone the diagnostic process and help define more accurately what is disorder and what is normal variation. The existing tests of brain function do not make this distinction.

Meanwhile, as parents, you have immediate concerns about a child who is suspected of, or diagnosed as, having ADHD. Until researchers nail down this issue, I have several suggestions:

- Every child suspected of having an attention problem should have a comprehensive, individual evaluation, including psychological testing conducted by an educational specialist. Tests can identify learning disabilities such as dyslexia or other information-processing problems. Keep in mind that no test can be given at this time to diagnose ADHD definitively. As yet, neurological examinations, EEGs (electroencephalograms), and PET (positron emission tomography) are inadequate for a diagnosis and therefore unnecessary.

- Parents should bring temperament into the discussion with teachers and others who think their child has ADHD. Consider what your child's temperament is and how it affects him and his caregivers. Share your observations of your child's temperament with teachers and discuss how to improve the fit in school. Consider if a poor fit with your child's temperament is the source of the problem. It may be.

- Parents should help children understand their own temperament differences. Unfortunately, as yet there are no books for children to help them with this process.

- Parents should discuss the current confusion about the vague criteria of ADHD if a professional diagnoses their child as having ADHD. Explain what you know about your child's temperament. Consider other factors, in addition to temperament, that may be contributing to inattentiveness, factors such as anxiety, depression, poor health, or inadequate motivation. Some professionals who understand temperament may reluctantly continue to use the ADHD label just to obtain insurance payments for services or to gain access to special education for your child.

- Finally—after the team of teacher, psychologist, and physician have consulted and reviewed your child's behavior and

school performance—if Ritalin or another stimulant is rec-
ommended to modify your child's attention problems, discuss the dosage of the medication, duration, and side effects
thoroughly with your child's doctor. Keep in mind that children without attention problems also perform better in
school with Ritalin, and therefore, the possible effectiveness
of the medication alone does not confirm a diagnosis of
ADHD. The medication usually does help children to be
more attentive in school; however, more importantly, they
will need special support in the classroom and behavioral
management at home. In other words, the pills may be helpful, but they are only part of the answer.

If you have been told that your child has ADHD, or someone suggests that he might have it, be aware of the controversy surrounding
this subject—and do not panic. Whether or not psychological testing identifies a learning disability, you should continue to take temperament into consideration in your daily interactions with your
child. Work with your child's teachers to reach a clear understanding
of his temperament and educational needs. Do not forget that most
of what is being called ADHD today is probably a display of normal
temperament differences that schools have trouble handling and is
not evidence of something wrong with your child's brain.

Until educators, physicians, and psychologists figure out a better
diagnostic system, you and your child will continue to be pioneers.
There is no clearly charted course at this time. Remember that you
are the expert on your own child. Trust yourself. You have more experience and knowledge about his behavioral style than anyone else has,
and you are in the position to help him improve the fit with his environment, even the school environment. Although you are not in the
classroom with him, you can work closely with his teachers to see
that he gets the understanding and support he needs. And, at home,
you can reinforce and encourage his achievements.

CHAPTER EIGHT

Reactions to Stress and Crisis

R uss and Andrea's marriage had crumbled into daily accusations and bitterness. They tried counseling, but it failed. Each called a divorce lawyer. Yet despite their antagonism toward each other, both parents were deeply concerned about the impact that separation and divorce would have on their children, seven-year-old Julie and five-year-old Josh.

Over the past few years, the children had seemed unhappy when their parents argued but revealed no signs of serious disturbance. That changed when Russ moved out of the house in the midst of a shouting match with Andrea.

Julie began asking her mother, almost daily, what would become of them "if Daddy doesn't come back." Julie, who had an "easy" temperament, did not weep or appear troubled. Andrea assumed that her daughter was not terribly upset.

Josh's reaction was quite different. Always more intense and negative when challenged by new situations, Josh did not adapt easily. He was much more obviously disturbed by his parents' situation. He often cried and wanted to sleep in his mother's bed. He whined about little things that normally did not bother him, such as running out of his favorite flavor of juice. His kindergarten teacher also noticed that he seemed unusually fretful and distractible.

Andrea and Russ thought that Julie "had her act together" and praised her for adjusting well to the pending divorce, and they felt angry at Josh for his reactions. They criticized every small annoying behavior and punished his greater *transgressions, such as his saying "I hate you," talking back, slamming doors, and refusing to do his household chores.*

As Josh's outbursts became more frequent, his parents decided to take him to a psychologist. By involving all four family members in the therapy sessions, the psychologist helped the parents better understand their children's reactions. The psychologist clarified for Andrea and Russ that Julie's surface reaction was a misleading indication of her underlying fears and distress. Ever the pleasant, easily adaptable child, Julie was really quite troubled by the family breakup. It was just not her style to respond dramatically to crises. The psychologist also pointed out that Josh was reacting more openly than his sister and in ways that were more irksome to his parents, although he was probably no more disturbed than Julie by the divorce. His parents' angry responses to him were making matters worse.

Once this information was out in the open, Andrea and Russ acknowledged their children's anxieties and reassured them that each parent would always continue to love them even if everyone did not live under the same roof. With time and ongoing emotional support from both parents, Julie was able to express and deal better with her worries, and Josh's behavior improved overall.

Children react in a variety of ways to stress and crisis, from daily hassles such as noisy neighbors and defective plumbing to major events such as the birth of a sibling; their parents' divorce; hospitalization or death of a loved one; starting a new school, camp, or college; violence in the home or community; family financial crisis; and even a natural disaster like a hurricane or flood.

Most children seem to be adversely affected by serious disruptions or social changes in their lives; however, each responds in her own individual way. A few children embrace new challenges—even those accompanied by stress. Other children appear to tolerate them satis-factorily but most feel threatened or upset by them.

General reactions typically include anxiety, depression, social withdrawal, poor schoolwork, or disturbances in sleeping, eating, or bladder and bowel control. Like adults, children also can develop post-traumatic stress disorder (PTSD). PTSD is a syndrome of spe-cific behavioral consequences, such as reliving the trauma but avoid-ing anything related to it, and some nonspecific disturbances, such as sleep disturbances and appetite loss, that appear after exposure to actual or threatened death or serious injury when the person has responded with intense fear, helplessness, or horror. The symptoms demonstrated by the individual child depend on several factors.

EFFECTS ON A CHILD'S REACTION TO CRISIS

A number of different influences shape a child's response to stress or crisis. Some of these factors can increase a child's vulnerability in stressful situations, whereas others can offer protection. If we learn to recognize these influences, we will be better able to understand a child's reactions.

One of the most important factors affecting a child's response is the crisis itself: its nature, intensity, duration, and disruptiveness. In Julie and Josh's case, the uprooting of their family, the departure of their father, and their uncertain future added up to a severe disloca-tion in their young lives. The long and drawn-out time beginning with their parents' months of arguments, through the separation, and up to the finalization of the divorce, made a tense situation worse.

The immediacy of the trauma itself can also determine its impact on children. For example, a child who has shared a close relationship with his grandfather will be more disturbed by his death than will another child who lives hundreds of miles away from his grandfather and has rarely visited him. Similarly, a child who watched as her family's home and possessions were damaged by a fire will be more upset than will the child who lives next door and only heard the fire sirens and smelled the smoke.

Emotional support is another significant factor affecting children's responses. If parents and other trusted adults are available and helpful during times of stress and crisis, the impact of the trauma can be cushioned. However, when a crisis leaves parents incapacitated, either physically or psychologically, they are less able to stabilize the child's life. Fortunately for Julie and Josh, their parents were able to see beyond their own problems and get therapy for the whole family.

Gender and age group differences have been reported by some studies on these reactions; however, the results are inconsistent and therefore not useful to us here.

We do know that temperament is an important factor contributing to a child's response to stress or crisis, although its role has not been widely studied in this area. But we have learned enough about it and the effects of temperament on other aspects of children's lives to conclude that it is a significant player in the nature and magnitude of their reactions to stressful events.

A child's style of reacting to stress makes a significant difference both in the experience itself and in the outcome for the child. Her sensitivity and reactivity contribute to her immediate response; her adaptability, mood, persistence, and other qualities shape the ongoing outcome. Let's consider what research shows.

In a study of 155 normal children who ranged in age from six to nine years, researchers found a connection between higher levels of stress and higher levels of behavioral problems. Eight of the nine more challenging temperament characteristics were found to be associated significantly with the development of those disturbances. Those traits were high activity, low adaptability, withdrawal from new stimuli, distractibility, high intensity, negative mood, low persistence, and irregularity. The children's preexisting temperaments were clearly involved in responses to diverse stresses ranging from everyday hassles to seriously disruptive life events.

In a study of children in South Carolina who experienced the devastation of Hurricane Hugo in 1989, investigators concluded that a child's immediate emotional reactions to that trauma may have been the most important factor for the development of symptoms of PTSD because they reflected the severity of the trauma, the temperament characteristics of the child, and the interaction between them. In other words, the reaction style the child has at the time of the crisis is an important factor in the later outcome.

Genetic contributions to reactions to stress have been assessed in twin studies even without identifying the responsible behavioral style differences. For example, a study of young adult male twins who served in Vietnam found evidence of a genetic influence in the development of PTSD. Even when differences in their combat experience were taken into consideration, genetic similarities predisposed some individuals to greater similarity of outcome, and genetic differences resulted in more diverse reactions. Identical twins were much more likely than were fraternal twins to exhibit the same degree of PTSD.

VARIOUS CRISES AND CHILDREN'S RESPONSES

Before we look at specific ways to help ease a child's adjustment to crises, let's consider the broad range of situations themselves, both common and rare.

ENTERING SCHOOL

One of the most common challenges early in life is starting school. Whether she started day care as an infant or stayed home until kindergarten, a child's first day in "real school" is a major milestone. Depending largely on their temperaments, individual children react differently to this new situation. Later on, the same challenge will reappear to a lesser extent each succeeding fall, especially during a transfer to another school. With many American families frequently moving to new locations, children are called on to adapt to unfamiliar schools, classmates, homes, and neighborhoods every few years.

SIBLING BIRTHS

As Chad illustrated in Chapter Four, most children are challenged whenever a new baby enters the home. The balance of relationships is suddenly tipped, and an only or older child is likely to receive less attention from his parents. For a long time, parents were blamed when older siblings did not adjust smoothly to the arrival of a sibling. Whether older children showed ambivalence, rivalry, or aggression toward the new baby, their reactions were traditionally attributed to the way that parents handled the situation.

Now we know that some of the reaction is attributable to the older child's innate temperament, rather than just the behaviors or attitudes learned from his parents.

Some psychologists have considered the birth of a baby brother or sister to be one of life's earliest and greatest crises. The research of Judith Dunn and her associates at Cambridge University in England, however, shows that children's reactions can vary widely. Their findings demonstrate that the differences in children's responses relate to their individual temperament traits before the new baby's arrival. The children who adapt easily to new circumstances and whose responses are generally positive, mild, and regular before the sibling's birth exhibit the same patterns when their siblings are born. Children with opposite temperaments are more likely to react with sleep problems, clingy behavior, and an absence of positive interest in the new baby.

Even as time passes, well after the infant has first arrived home, temperament traits continue to influence how the older children interact with both their mothers and new siblings. Children with low adaptability and high intensity tend to protest more while Mom is caring for the baby and are less likely to ignore these activities. These older siblings often suck their thumbs or hold their favorite stuffed animal or blanket for comfort as they watch her bathing or feeding their new brother or sister.

SEPARATION, DIVORCE, AND REMARRIAGE

About half the marriages in the United States end in divorce. The degree of stress that children experience from this family disruption reflects the following: the intensity of parental fighting that has preceded the divorce; the amount of emotional support the child receives throughout this difficult period; the child's own temperament; and other factors such as age, gender, and intelligence.

Research studies have shown, for instance, that intelligent children are more resilient and older children are more disturbed by their parents' breakup. Boys have been shown to be affected more negatively than girls by divorce and by life in a one-parent household where the mother has custody; however, girls have more long-term difficulty in adjusting to a stepfather.

One of the few studies that has looked at temperament characteristics of children of divorce was based on nurses' ratings of behavior at well-child medical visits during the first two years of life. Traits such as irritability, soothability, activity, sociability, and regularity were considered for their roles either in protecting children from the throes of divorce or in making them more vulnerable to such upheaval in their lives.

The study concluded that, when mothers were especially stressed, children with the more challenging temperament traits were more likely to evoke unpleasant reactions from their mothers and become the target for them. These children were less able to cope with both the general situation and with angry responses from their stressed parents.

In the highly charged atmosphere of separation and divorce, it can be difficult to sort out the causes of a child's negative reactions and behaviors. Are outbursts such as Josh's, as described earlier in this chapter, a result of the stressful events (in that case, his parents' arguments and his father's moving out of the house)? Or are they manifestations of his predisposing traits, such as low adaptability and negative mood? Probably both. Undoubtedly, a network of factors is interacting whenever a family is pulled apart. Even if the cause and role of each factor are not clear, we need to consider the child's temperament before the separation and divorce if we are to help the child through this crisis.

Beyond what has been demonstrated by research, some tentative conclusions are reasonable. Children are probably always affected by divorce. The more parental tension and fighting, the more behavioral and emotional disruption will be evident in the children. Under heavy stresses of their own, parents may be inconsistent about their expectations of and attitudes toward their children. This can be especially hard on children who do not adapt easily. More than others, these children need consistency, particularly during periods of stress and crisis. Living conditions can become even more unpredictable when parents maintain two separate households in which rules and regulations differ. Visitation arrangements can compound the stress if both parents fall into the trap of putting their children in the middle of their own strife or using them as tools of revenge against the other parent.

After the divorce is final, some parents expect their children to accept the fact and get on with their lives. Yet other challenges arise that call for the children to adapt: A parent who had more time for them in the past is now a single parent more heavily burdened with raising children, earning a living, and running the household alone; or there may be a new stepparent or stepsiblings to get along with. For children who do not adapt easily, who are withdrawing in new situations, who need regularity in their routines, or whose moods tend to be negative, the stresses of a divorce and its aftermath require extra attention and careful management.

FOSTER AND ADOPTIVE PLACEMENT

Infants and children who are placed in foster care or who are adopted may experience unusual stress in adjusting to a new family life. About 2 percent of children in America are adopted and more than half a million are in foster care. These children have the same range of temperament traits as other children and, similarly, they need the help of the adults in their lives to ensure a good fit between their temperaments and their new family environments.

A study of children placed in foster care showed that certain traits predict outcome: An inflexible mother and a child with negative mood or low regularity, for example, produce more conflict, lower parental satisfaction, and poorer placement success, as judged by the placement agency.

In helping foster or adoptive children, it is important to recognize temperament as a contributing factor to their adjustment. When negative reactions or behaviors arise, it should not be assumed that they are necessarily the fault of the child or the adoptive or foster parents; the child's temperament and the parent–child fit should also be considered. If concerns exist about the behavior of a child being placed for foster care or adoption, the placement agency should provide diagnostic services to distinguish temperament issues such as low adaptability or negative mood from such behavioral or emotional problems as oppositional behavior or depression.

DISASTERS AND OTHER CRISES

Street violence, automobile crashes, fires, hurricanes, earthquakes, floods—any of these horrors are critical events in the life of a child. Many studies have documented the impact these events have on children. But the role of temperament—and whether it makes some children more or less vulnerable than others—has not been as widely assessed.

When appropriate studies are done, the role of temperament will undoubtedly be found to influence a child's reaction to a parent's illness, hospitalization, or death; family separations; geographical moves; and family, neighborhood, civil violence, and war. As we await this research, we can assume that temperament probably matters here, too.

WHAT TO DO

Stress and crisis cannot be avoided. Life without them, although it would be more peaceful, is hard to imagine. Some would argue that stress and crisis, as trying as they can sometimes be, can strengthen people in the long run. Children and adults can learn and grow from them, but only under certain limited circumstances.

Children usually cannot get through stressful experiences alone. Some can handle them better than others can; however, all children need support and understanding in the midst of crisis and during its aftermath. There are several steps that parents can take to help children of all temperaments get through tough times.

- *Prepare for crisis.* If you are planning to move to a new community, divorce your spouse, adopt another child, enter the hospital, attend a funeral of a loved one, or bring any significant change into your family life, talk with your children about it in advance. Do not pull any surprises. Listen to their concerns, acknowledge their fears and apprehensions, and answer their questions as honestly as you can. Reassure them, and give them the facts about the situation in a clear and age-appropriate way.

- *Provide support.* Whether or not a crisis can be anticipated and prepared for, children will need support as they are going through it. Parents can help children by stabilizing their lives and cushioning them from the worst of the trauma. Even after moving out, Russ continued to be involved with Julie and Josh's care. Children should be given opportunities to talk about the situation and their emotions and to express their anger or frustrations in ways that do not harm themselves or others. Parents can teach specific coping skills with useful activities, such as involving an older sibling in the care of a newborn. Parents also can advise children about prioritizing by helping them determine which of the current disruptions to ignore for the moment. It is, of course, particularly hard for parents to provide support when they themselves are involved in the crisis.

- *Monitor your child's reactions.* By now you know a great deal about the role temperament plays in various aspects of your child's life. As you watch the outward expressions of how your child is coping with a crisis, keep Josh and Julie in mind. Remember that different temperaments influence behaviors when children are under unusual stress. Josh and Julie were about equally upset by their parents' divorce but both children exhibited their reactions differently. When a crisis arises, bring your child's temperament into the picture, and try to separate normal, expected reactions from exaggerated ones, such as those of Josh, and underexpressed ones, such as those of Julie.

- *Seek emotional support from family, friends, and community.* What better time to reach out to aunts, uncles, and grandparents? Parents cannot always do it alone. Andrea's parents lived nearby and often entertained Julie and Josh and took care of them when sickness kept them home from school. If a crisis is pending, ask for help to minimize the impact and get through it for yourself and your children. If the crisis is sudden or unexpected, even more emotional support will be necessary. When you call on others for help, ask them to pay particular attention to your child's individual temperamental needs. If she is shy, make sure friends and family know this and that she may be even more withdrawn in the face of this crisis. If he does not adapt easily to strange situations, let them know that, too, and suggest that others extend an extra measure of patience during this stressful period. If she is pleasant and adaptable, beware of underestimating the degree of disturbance.

- *Find professional help when necessary.* You know your child's style of reacting to new situations quite well by now. You are probably able to distinguish, even in a crisis, whether her behavior is what would be expected in this situation or whether it is magnified or diminished by her particular behavioral style traits. If your child appears to be having serious problems coping with the crisis at hand, and if you are so affected by it that you are having difficulty yourself, it is important to seek professional counseling. Talk with your child's pediatrician, your family physician, or a mental health professional or agency if you cannot handle it yourself. Do not add another weight to your shoulders by trying to do it all alone.

CHAPTER NINE

Toward More Effective and Rewarding Parenthood

As you approach the end of this book, you should congratulate yourself for taking the time and making the effort to learn more about temperament, the ways it affects you, and its contributions to your child's social behavior, development, school performance, physical health, and responses to stressors in the environment.

You have acquired insights about temperament that most parents and many professionals do not yet have. You know that it is perfectly normal for children to exhibit wide variations in behavioral style. You have observed your children in many circumstances and have profiled their individual temperament characteristics. You have thought about how your child's temperament affects you as an adult and as a parent. And you have probably started to rethink your responses to your child in various circumstances and have revised some of those responses to increase harmony and decrease unnecessary conflict in your family's day-to-day life.

You are already ahead of the game. Most parents have the ability to become more competent and satisfied, and the vast majority of parents have the will to do so. Ability and inclination, however, are not always enough. Knowledge and specific skills are also necessary if parents are to help children grow and adjust to new challenges, improve their interactions with other people, and feel confident about themselves.

Even though you have come this far, there is more work to do. Although your child's temperament will not change very much, circumstances are always shifting and presenting new issues of fit. Your child will continue to bring you new challenges, adventures, and problems that will test your skills. One of the many wonderful things about children is that they are always giving parents new opportunities to learn. We teach them, but they constantly teach us about ourselves and themselves. Although we may not always rise to the challenge as successfully as we would wish, our children will always give us another chance to practice tomorrow, next week, or next year.

Whether your child is a baby or a teenager, you can start right away to use this information and these new approaches to achieving a good fit. Ideally, parents can begin raising children from infancy with the benefit of knowing more about temperament. Even if your children are older, you still will be able to apply the principles outlined in this book. It is never too late.

As new dilemmas arise, you will be more alert to the influences of your child's temperament. You will be able to see more accurately just why your child is reacting in a particular way. Your knowledge will help you manage behavior in ways that can alleviate some of the strain and promote better harmony. You will feel, and rightly so, that you are a more competent parent.

Before you close these covers, let's briefly reconsider what we know about temperament differences in children and how this information can improve our relations with them and help them cope with ever-new challenges.

Immediately following this review is a series of frequently asked questions. These questions and the answers to them serve a dual purpose. They summarize some points made earlier in the book, and therefore provide an easy, accessible way for you to return to this material later on, perhaps when your child is a little older or when you encounter a new issue. They also discuss some common confusions about temperament and related topics that did not merit full explanation in earlier chapters. Nonetheless, parents may still raise some of these questions even after they have learned a great deal about temperament, and therefore, we feel they deserve to be answered and put into context.

WHAT WE KNOW

Although temperament certainly does not explain all the mysteries of life, we do have reason to celebrate the new information about it that has become known in the years since the early 1960s. This information, which we have tried to make as available and clear as possible through these pages, can help improve everyone's parenting skills. And these skills should lead parents to feel greater satisfaction and confidence in themselves, which ultimately benefits their children.

Thanks to recent research, we now recognize that temperament differences in children are very real. They are not merely "perceptions" or something imagined by parents or other adults. Children are born with these variations in style of reacting to change, stress, and ordinary events. About 50 percent of temperament is determined by heredity, with the rest coming from the environment and a child's own physical and developmental status. Temperament traits seem to be increasingly stable at least up through the elementary school years, as far as they have been tracked so far, and probably remain fairly consistent into adolescence and adulthood.

We also know that temperament differences are vitally important both to children and to their caregivers. Earlier chapters have shown the multitude of ways that temperament interactions affect health, development, social behavior, academic performance, and response to stress and crisis. We know that children's behavioral styles influence parents and other adults both as persons and as caregivers who are responsible for providing children with physical, developmental, behavioral, and socialization needs.

One of the most important results of research has been a clearer distinction between normal temperament variations and behavioral problems, because their management should be quite different. Too many children have been criticized, labeled, reprimanded, punished, isolated, ostracized, or otherwise harmed for behaviors that were expressions of their temperament—a temperament that was in conflict with a particular setting. A shy child was scolded for not participating in a group event. A stubborn child was forced into an activity that he strongly resisted.

Such children were seen as having behavioral problems before their innate temperaments were ever considered. Although their behaviors may be bothersome to parents and other caregivers, few have, until now, taken temperament into account in trying to manage children's behavior. Now, with a better understanding of temperament characteristics, parents can accommodate their children in ways that improve the fit between them. Parents can decrease conflict and stress while at the same time guide their children toward a healthy behavioral adjustment.

Once temperament traits are identified and assessed (and distinguished from behavioral adjustment problems such as aggressiveness or poor self-esteem), most issues of fit can be managed successfully by parents without professional help. You learned how to profile your child's temperament in Chapter One. As your children grow up, from time to time you may want to refer back to the notes you made when reading that chapter and make new observations. The traits may change or, even if they stay the same, their importance to you or your child may increase or decrease.

Parents have probably always recognized—deep down—their child's unique, individual temperament; however, books, "busybody" neighbors, and authorities who appear on talk shows may have shaken their confidence. Others may have led parents to believe that all children should react and respond in particular ways. If a child deviates from "the norm," by being more boisterous, or timid, or irregular about her daily rhythms than most children, then there must be something wrong with her—or so goes this line of thinking.

Now parents who have recognized different temperament styles can be reassured that *this variation is normal.* Many professionals are now reinforcing parents' intuitive, practical good sense. At last!

Although we have learned a great deal about temperament since the 1960s, there is still much to discover. For the moment, it may be useful to recognize the limits of our information so that no one will assume that temperament is responsible for every complexity in life. The fact of a major genetic contribution to temperament has been established; however, the details are still elusive. How many genes are involved and on which chromosomes are they to be found? When and how are they turned on and off? At what times do they exercise their greatest and least influence? Is there any way to predict from parents just what sort of temperament a child will have?

What are the principal nongenetic influences? When and how do they make themselves felt most strongly? Just how long lasting, for example, are the effects of various foods and drugs that the baby comes in contact with while in the womb? Again, we have much more to discover.

Temperament traits are never completely fixed, nor are they completely changeable. Although we do know that temperament is fairly stable, we do not know which traits show the earliest, strongest, and most enduring stability. How and why do changes occur?

We also need to learn more about the distinction between normal variations of two specific temperament traits, inattentiveness and activity, and similar but possibly abnormal attention deficit/ hyperactivity disorder behaviors that some think are evidence of subtle brain malfunction, now referred to as ADHD.

FREQUENTLY ASKED QUESTIONS ABOUT TEMPERAMENT

What is the relationship between temperament and intelligence? Aren't adaptable children smarter?

Intelligence and adaptability are similar; however, they are different, separate parts of personality. Intelligence concerns the ability to learn and to apply what you have learned, to understand and think rationally. Adaptability is the ease of being changed or of changing yourself in some desirable direction.

A child may be bright but not adaptable, or adaptable but not bright. There does seem to be some overlap between intelligence and adaptability, according to some studies, because the process of adaptation appears to some extent to be affected by an individual's intelligence. Smarter people, for example, may adapt faster under some circumstances. There is another consideration: Attentive and adaptable children may be more skillful at taking IQ tests, and therefore may be considered more intelligent. High adaptability also may make a child seem more intelligent than he is. There is still much to be learned about the relationship between intelligence and adaptability.

What about introversion and extroversion? Are they parts of temperament?

These dimensions of personality concern the degree of comfort people feel in social situations and the direction in which they prefer to focus their energies. An introverted personality prefers to direct energies inward toward the self rather than outward toward the external world. An introvert tends to be more satisfied with his own thoughts and amusements than with those of other people. An extrovert finds more satisfaction in other people and external things.

Although there is some debate on this matter, these popular terms probably refer more to an aspect of behavioral adjustment than to inborn temperament or behavioral style traits. However, we may guess that temperament is a major determinant of introversion and extroversion. It makes sense, for example, that less sociable children (those with more timid initial reaction and lower adaptability) would be more likely to become introverted, but this is not necessarily so.

What is meant by an "artistic temperament"? A "judicial temperament"?

We often hear opinions that certain temperaments are more common in, or better suited to, certain occupations. The stereotype of the artistic temperament is said to be one of sensitivity, intensity, and unpredictability, but also of great persistence at times. A judicial temperament is popularly described as one of low "arousability," or perhaps low intensity, and high attention span, which are traits that can be the stuff of which good lawyers and judges are made.

I am unaware of any studies that have examined the nine dimensions of temperament among artists, attorneys, and judges. I, however, am of the opinion that there is not just one, but a great variety of temperaments that are compatible with just about any line of work. Success in any occupation is not just a matter of temperament; it requires other features such as appropriate mental abilities, motivation, and opportunities. For example, among the professionally and personally competent physicians I have known, I have observed a broad range of temperaments.

What about impulsivity as a temperament trait?

Impulsivity is a frequently heard term applied to the rate at which a child translates thoughts or feelings into action. The impulsive child acts rapidly without hesitation, whereas the less impulsive one acts more slowly after considering the outcome or consequences.

Should impulsivity be one of the basic temperament traits? Twenty years ago, Robert Plomin, one of the leading temperament researchers, included it as one of four traits, but he later decided to withdraw it because of lack of evidence that there is any hereditary basis for it. Some other researchers have argued that it is not necessary to prove heredity to establish a trait as temperament.

The final answer is not yet available, but we can postulate that impulsivity is more a part of behavioral adjustment than a primary, inborn temperament trait. Perhaps initial reaction and intensity and some other temperament characteristics contribute to impulsivity to some degree, but it seems probable that the establishment of impulse control lies as much—or more—in the degree to which caregivers train children to restrain themselves. Impulse control is probably better learned through early interactions (including prevention and modeling by parents) than by attempts at later revisions. Some parents are better teachers than others are, and some children more easily taught. The issue of impulsivity in ADHD was discussed in Chapter Eight.

What do horoscopes tell us about temperament? Is there any truth to them?

Astrology, the art of attempting to predict the future by the relative positions of heavenly bodies, dates back to ancient Babylon. Astrologers believe that a person's horoscope influences personality and life course. Despite their popularity, horoscopes have no scientific merit whatsoever and should not be taken seriously. That many people continue to consult them probably has much to do with the ever-present uncertainty about the future. Many people will take any guidance and comfort they can find to reduce their anxiety.

If temperament is partly determined by genetics, why are parents often so different from their children and siblings so different from each other?

Our understanding of the genetic influence on temperament comes mainly from studying similarities between twins, not between the generations. There must be similarities between parents and children, but so far they have not been adequately determined. We have to say that we do not know, at the present time, how to predict what sort of temperament a child of two particular parents will have. This is not a simple pattern of inheritance such as eye color. Undoubtedly there are many genes involved in the transmission of temperament, and we do not know which ones will go to one child and which others may turn up in the next child, or the child after that one. We should remember that physical and environmental differences begin to mold the basic genetic pattern right from the start.

If temperament is genetically determined, why is it not most obvious in newborns? Why does the genetic influence increase with time?

Because genes are in the body from the moment of conception and the external social environment has not made much of an impact on a baby before birth, you might think that you would see the genes expressed most clearly in the newborn period. However, it seems that things do not work in that way. Apparently, the main factors that determine behavioral differences at birth are the physical status of the mother during pregnancy and the conditions during labor and delivery. The effects of the genes are either weakly expressed right after birth, or they are overwhelmed by the temporary effects of pregnancy and delivery.

Genetic influences become more evident as the child grows older and has had more chance to be influenced by the impact of genes on the brain, which is rapidly growing and maturing in the first year of life. Consider a similar situation with physical growth. How big a baby is at birth is determined as much by the nutritional state of the mother during pregnancy and the duration of the pregnancy as it is by genes. The genes for body size are poorly expressed at birth and do not become highly evident until the second year of life. From then on, they continue to be very important to the extent that a child's adult height can be predicted with some accuracy from age two by knowing the height of the mother and father.

If a child's temperament changes during the first few weeks or months, is it the parent's fault?

We do not know exactly how temperament changes over the first few months of life. Surprisingly enough, this critical period of life is one of the least well studied. As far as we know, shifts in a baby's temperament are not anyone's fault.

We do believe that two factors are operating: a wearing off of the temporary effects on behavior caused by the pregnancy and delivery experience and the increasing expression of the child's genes. At this point, we cannot say for certain that parents either do or do not modify the baby's temperament by the way they handle him during these early weeks and months. However, parents' management of the infant will influence the presence or absence of those clinical concerns (such as excessive crying, sleep problems, and overfeeding) that are related to their interaction with the baby's temperament.

Some people say that you can tell the difference between inborn and acquired shyness by eye color, the shape of the face, and other physical traits. Is this true?

One research group has reported that children who display shyness early in life, and who are believed to be that way because of an inborn tendency, may have some physical differences from those who become shy as a result of experiences after birth. These findings are too preliminary and uncertain to be useful for making such distinctions.

It is simpler to make your own observations about when your child became shy. If it is inborn temperament, you can trace it back to very early times when your child first became aware of unfamiliar people, foods, and places. If the shyness has come on later, perhaps following some frightening experience, there is usually an obvious turning point or change that you can pinpoint.

Do the mother's feelings during pregnancy have an impact on a child's temperament?

A great deal of folklore exists about the way a mother's feelings during pregnancy influence the behavior of a baby after birth. A few studies have documented that some of these emotions do have an impact on the baby in the period immediately after birth. However, no study has investigated the unlikely possibility that these newborn differences may persist beyond this point.

What about the influence on temperament if a mother used drugs during pregnancy?

This subject is being investigated extensively, especially the use of alcohol, cocaine, and cigarettes. The conclusions reached so far are confusing. We know that these substances are not good for the health of children and adults; however, the question of lasting effects from maternal use during pregnancy has been very difficult to answer. Often, more than one potentially harmful substance has been used and might be responsible for any observed problems in the child. Malnutrition and various social stressors may add to the difficulty in separating specific cause-and-effect relationships. Substances may be taken in differing amounts, at different times, and for different lengths of time. Even when unborn babies are apparently exposed to the same amount of a particular substance, they may experience a range of outcomes.

There is some agreement that infants with fetal alcohol syndrome (a set of physical and developmental defects related to the mother's fairly heavy use of alcohol during her pregnancy) also tend to be more irritable during infancy and to have trouble with attention in their school years. Otherwise consistent, lasting differences are difficult to determine. A minority of newborns who have been exposed to cocaine *in utero* have disruptions of sleep patterns, tremors, feeding problems, irritability, and sometimes convulsions. The outcome of all this is so variable that we cannot responsibly make predictions of what the child will be like months or years later.

How likely is it that a "difficult" infant will become "easier"?

Fortunately, we can say that most difficult infants do become easier as they go through the first several years. Research has shown that most actually become easier both by objective measurement of temperament characteristics (as determined by professionals' standardized questionnaires) and by parents' perceptions or overall judgments. Those youngsters who do remain objectively hard to manage (with traits of low adaptability and negative mood, for example) are frequently regarded as less challenging because their parents have learned to understand what is going on and have found ways to improve the fit and diminish the stress. But unfortunately, some remain hard to manage.

Is it true that many children become more difficult at around the age of two?

It is true that a few children do develop more of these traits (less flexibility, more negative mood, and so on) that make them more challenging to care for. The reasons for this is not very well understood. A more likely explanation for such toddlers, seeming to be harder to manage is that their parents did not realize how normal toddlers actually behave. (Seeking more independence and autonomy is typical of toddlers).

Another explanation may be that some aspect of the same temperament pattern that was once acceptable to the parents has now become annoying. A common example is the highly active infant who, when she was in the crib or playpen, did not present much of a problem. Once she became a toddler and learned to walk, however, her parents were always on edge because she seemed to be in constant motion. Similarly, as two-year-olds begin to talk more, traits such as low adaptability or slowness to warm up in unfamiliar situations are now expressed for the first time with words—usually "No! I don't want to."

What about birth order? Is it true that firstborn children generally are more difficult than subsequent children are? Or is it true that the second child is more of a problem?

Greater difficulty is probably in the eye of the beholder. Currently available data indicate that firstborn children are no more likely to be fussy and inflexible than are their siblings. Likewise, secondborn children are no harder to get along with than others.

The firstborn child may seem challenging to manage to parents who are inexperienced and do not always know what to expect of their child's behavior. Conversely, first-time parents may regard their child as perfect, only later to become more realistic about, or even critical of, their next child.

If my first child is fairly difficult, what are the chances of the next one, or two, being that way?

Studies show that 5 to 15 percent of infants and toddlers are regarded by their parents as being especially hard to manage. Having already had this experience once does not mean that you are either more or less likely to have it again. The one-in-ten odds will be about the same, which means that you probably will not have a hard-to-manage child next time.

How different are the temperaments of boys and girls? Are some differences learned? Are there genetic differences between them? Are boys more active? Are girls shyer?

Most of us have been brought up with the idea that girls and boys are different in many ways, including temperament. With such a strong, known influence of genes on temperament, we might expect that formal studies would confirm our beliefs about these gender differences.

Through age 12, boys and girls are quite similar when it comes to temperament, although they may be different in other ways. Young girls have been shown to be a little more timid than boys, and boys appear to be a little more active than girls. A few other minor differences also have been demonstrated. In other words, the differences *within* any group of boys and the differences *within* any group of girls are far greater than the differences *between* the two gender groups.

What happens to these differences during and after puberty has not been studied sufficiently. If at this time they are determined to have grown significantly dissimilar, researchers must then try to establish how much of this difference has a physical or temperamental basis and how much is caused by adolescents trying to live up to the expectations for behavior imposed on them by their social peers and by adults.

What is the effect of artificial food colorings and flavors, and sugar, on temperament?

Over twenty years ago an allergist in California, Benjamin Feingold, aroused a great deal of concern across the country by urging the view that chemical additives in food are responsible for a variety of behavioral changes, including "hyperactivity." Similar doubts have been raised by others concerning the unfavorable effects of sugar and the artificial sweetener aspartame (Nutrasweet). None of these claims has stood up to rigorous scientific testing. Perhaps, it was all a matter of the power of suggestion. There may be a rare child who is truly intolerant of a specific food ingredient and should avoid it, which does not mean that all children need to have that particular food removed from their diets.

Nevertheless, it is important to make sure your child has a wholesome diet and to keep your eyes open for responsible reports of possible harm from food additives. If you are confused by reports in the popular media, consult your child's doctor.

Are race and ethnicity related to differences in temperament? Examples are the intense Mediterranean or the reserved Scandinavian stereotypes.

We are all aware of popular notions that certain racial or ethnic groups are thought to be more unpredictable, gloomy, intense, persistent, sensitive, and so on. And sooner or later, just about every group is accused of being too stubborn.

If these differences really do exist, they are very hard to measure accurately. If variations between population groups could somehow be established, then we would try to figure out whether they are inherited or passed on to children by the different cultures in which they live. Such a separation would be very difficult to accomplish. For the time being, it seems wise to conclude that such differences have been neither proved nor disproved.

Can a child's temperament be changed in a major way by good or bad experiences?

No reliable scientific data exist to answer that question; however, it does seem logical to assume that a child who is treated with affection and reasonable discipline will maintain and possibly increase a tendency to react with a positive mood and flexibility, thus possibly lessening the reactions of negative mood and inflexibility.

On the other hand, if a child is continually exposed to very frightening or unpleasant circumstances, he is likely to move in the opposite direction. Less desirable traits such as inflexibility may be reinforced by inappropriate parental tolerance or encouragement, and more desirable traits may decrease.

Can a child's temperament be changed by psychotherapy?

Although no research exists to answer this important question, it seems unlikely that talking or playing with a child in a certain way, even when done at great length, will alter traits that are largely genetically determined. However, the child may learn to develop a conscious suppression of some of the less adaptive traits, or to develop strategies for easing the fit with his environment.

Do drugs change temperament?

Ritalin (methylphenidate) has been reported to increase attention and decrease activity in some children diagnosed with ADHD. It is widely assumed that the effect of the drug is to correct some malfunction in the child's brain. Stimulants of the brain, however, have also been shown to improve these functions in completely normal children. It therefore may be that the child's temperament is being temporarily altered by the drug. Use of other drugs, such as Prozac (fluoxetine), is likely to be considered in the near future.

How can a doctor correctly judge my child's temperament or behavior when her behavior is so different in the doctor's office from her behavior at home or school?

Your child's medical doctor should not depend merely on what he or she sees during the brief ten- to twenty-minute office visit. A child's behavior in the office can be better or worse, or simply different, from the behavior you observe at home or the teacher reports from school. You can help the doctor by indicating how typical your child's performance in the doctor's office is in comparison with what happens at home and at school. In judging your child, the physician should depend on reports from you, the parent, and from teachers and other caregivers.

When father and mother disagree about the child's temperament, who is right?

Whenever two people make independent observations of the same person, thing, or event, their reports almost always differ, at least a little. Even physicists separately measuring identical objects and events with precise tools produce results with slight differences.

With something as complex as human behavior, we have to expect greater variations between what one person and another observes and reports. Although parents generally agree about their child's behavior, it is not unusual for them to vary and disagree to some extent. The variation may result from each parent's seeing the child at different times of the day or for different lengths of time. A child may actually respond differently to each parent. The most important factor is probably that the mother, even when working outside the home, usually spends more time with the child than the father does in most families.

When there is disagreement, who is right? Parents should try to pool their observations, discuss them, and try to reach a mutual understanding of their child's temperament and behavior. Only by this collaborative process can you design a coherent, consistent management plan. Some of the most troublesome disciplinary problems arise when a child picks up conflicting messages from parents.

After only a few minutes with my child, my friend made a judgment about her with which I disagree. Who is right?

Although not dependable, snap judgments are sometimes accurate. We tend to accept the hasty judgments of others when they agree with our own (for example, "He's such a pleasant child."). However, we should be hesitant to do so. When the snap judgment disagrees with our own (for example, "He's too active."), the best course may be to ask the person to explain how he arrived at that conclusion, ask for opinions of others whose judgment you respect, or make further observations on your own and compare them with other children to see whether there is any merit in your friend's opinion. If these cast doubt on your friend's judgment, then you can safely ignore it. Although your friend may have a fresh perspective, you know your child better.

The day care staff presents a different picture of my child from what we see at home. Do they really understand my child as well as I do?

Sometimes children actually do behave differently at home than they do at school or day care. Their experiences in the two settings may bring out different sides of the child's repertory of behavioral reactions.

A transformation is also commonly observed when children put on their best behavior in public but then come home and "let it all hang out," displaying their less pleasant or flexible sides to their family.

Another possible explanation is that in a day care center or school, child care specialists are often more experienced at watching and evaluating children's behavior than most parents are. As a result, they may have made some significant observations that parents have missed. These observations could help parents understand their child better.

Parents should always take the reports of day care workers and teachers' seriously, whether they agree or conflict with observations made at home. Parent–teacher conferences held on a regular basis are helpful for both sides to share their views.

I have heard about ways to measure personality, such as the Myers-Briggs classification system. Is there a relationship between these and temperament ratings?

The Myers-Briggs Type Indicator is a method for adults to rate their own personalities in four areas: introversion–extroversion, processes of perception, processes of judgment, and attitudes toward the outside world. These criteria are reported to be helpful to adults in achieving an understanding of their personalities and for counselors trying to help them.

The criteria may turn out to be related to temperament to some degree; however, the four areas are not themselves temperament traits as we define the term. They have more to do with thinking than with behaving. And they have not been adapted for use in children.

The Thorndike Dimensions of Temperament Scale is a system specifically designed for assessing adult temperament. Its dimensions, such as active–lethargic and placid–irritable, are closer to those we have been using. Some researchers also have successfully applied the same nine traits that we have been describing in this book to assess adult temperament.

Is it true that children really cannot help how their temperaments are, meaning they are not that way on purpose?

A child's temperament is the way he or she starts responding to people and situations when very young. These reactions are what come to the child immediately, before there is time to reflect on the full meaning or consequences of the reaction. An intense child, for example, is intense not because he has thought the matter through and decided that a particular situation calls for loud, dramatic, or passionate response. His intense response is what comes naturally to him, without conscious thought.

As the child grows older, he may consciously and deliberately moderate some temperament traits either by encouraging them or by trying to suppress them. The intense child may discover that explosive reactions help him to get his way, and so he cultivates his intensity. If he finds himself being sharply criticized for his intensity, he may try to curb his explosive reactions or tone them down. With older children, in whom we see an increasing awareness of and ability to control the expression of temperament, we can say that they can be held more responsible for these expressions, although not for their underlying tendencies.

My child's pediatrician does not believe in temperament. He says that I made my child whiny, stubborn, and overly active by the way I raised her. What should I do?

Many family physicians and pediatricians—as well as many psychologists, teachers, and social workers—are deficient in the knowledge of temperament research. The new information available in this and other books and journals may not have reached them because they are so busy keeping up with vast new developments in other matters and with ever-growing mountains of paperwork.

Two steps are possible for you to take. You can share your insights about your child's temperament with the doctor and demonstrate how helpful you find them to be. You also can present the doctor (or the teacher, counselor, or whomever) with some authoritative reading matter that you believe to be instructive at a professional level. If this can be done as an act of respect, rather than one of criticism, the doctor will probably be grateful to you.

The doctor says my child will grow out of his current behavior. Is this possible?

Doctors have often been criticized for telling parents that their child will, in time, stop certain behaviors that annoy or upset them. We should acknowledge that this is true to some extent. Children do stop sucking their thumbs and wetting their beds. But we cannot count on just the passage of time to erase a behavioral problem such as aggressiveness or an emotional problem such as depression.

There is no certainty that annoying temperament traits will disappear or become less bothersome if only we wait long enough. If your child has temperament traits that are producing stress in your relationship with her, the only reasonable approach is to identify the traits, understand where they come from, and plan better tactics for handling them so that the conflict and stress are reduced.

Our doctor will not arrange to have further evaluations performed of worrisome behaviors, but teachers are pushing us for more tests. What should we do?

This is a distressing situation for parents caught in the middle of different professional opinions. Be sure that you have made it clear to the doctor how concerned you (and the teachers) are about the behaviors and that the doctor has done everything possible aside from referring your child to another professional. Perhaps a longer office visit or just another short visit can be arranged to discuss and resolve the problem. Also, make sure that you have fully understood the doctor's response to your expressed concern and the reasons for it. It may be that further examinations are not needed. All children with headaches, for instance, do not need brain scans, and all timid children do not need psychotherapy.

If after all of this your child provides clear indications for further advice or services, consider arranging them yourself through a parents' self-help group or with appropriate medical or psychological services outside your immediate healthcare network. This can be complicated, time-consuming, and expensive in these days of managed care. Do not change doctors impulsively; your doctor may indeed be correct; however, trust yourself if you are still worried.

My child is so difficult that I cannot imagine any situation in which there would be a good "fit." What is the solution?

The discussion of good and poor "fit" has misled some people into thinking that it is always possible to find a way to adjust the environment so that the child and caregiver suit each other with no friction and with complete comfort. A good fit occurs when the values and expectations of parents and other caregivers in the environment are in accord with the capacities and temperament of the child. A good fit does not mean a complete lack of stress and conflict. Some of these uncomfortable feelings are inevitable in normal development.

What you should be trying to achieve is a maximum reduction of the stress and conflict to the point where life is reasonably smooth for your child and you. This can be accomplished, at least part of the time, with any temperament traits. Friction with even the most challenging child can be reduced to levels that are bearable for most parents. And all children have at least brief periods when they are quite pleasant and lovable. We should make the most of these times when they occur and hope that they will become longer and more frequent.

I worry that all this trouble managing my child stems from my returning to full-time work. Could that be true?

Many parents worry that returning to work when the child is young—or, conversely, staying home with children until thcy cnter school—is the cause of behavior or emotional problems. Remember that your return to work or your decision to stay at home has not altered your child's temperament. She has not become more intense or shy or irregular or sensitive because of your work status.

What may have changed is your relationship with her. Are you spending less time with her? Are you more hurried and tired? Are you feeling guilty about giving her less time and attention, and therefore, are you having trouble setting limits on her unacceptable behaviors? Are you angry or conflicted about putting your career on hold and consequently allowing your feelings to affect your interactions with her?

Any of these alterations in the way you interact with your child may be disruptive to her behavioral adjustment. You can avoid these problems if you try to maintain as normal and consistent a relationship with her as possible.

Are "difficult" children the only ones at risk of clinical or emotional problems because of their temperaments?

Children with withdrawing initial reactions, slow adaptability, extensive negativity in responses, and intensity— singly or together in a cluster—have been demonstrated to be particularly at risk for developing social behavioral problems, at least in a society such as ours. However, any temperament traits or clusters of traits can be risk factors if they predispose a child to a poor fit with his particular environment, to excessive stress and conflict in the relationships with parents and other caregivers, and to clinical problems in his physical health, development, or behavior. Sometimes high activity, for example, makes for a good fit and sometimes for a poor fit; it depends on the requirements of the specific environment. The same can be said for low activity and for all other traits.

Why does his father have so little problem managing him when I am having such a tough time with our son?

There could be several possible explanations. It may be that he simply does not have as many significant, stressful contacts with your child as you have. Which parent has more interaction with your son at hurried, tense times such as rushing to get ready for school, trips to the doctor, or when he comes home tired or grumpy from school?

It could be that his father is more of a stern authority whom your child is more likely to obey. Or Dad may simply give him clearer directions. The main explanation to consider carefully is whether Dad may have actually figured out some ways of handling your son that you might understand and copy: more patience at a crucial time, not responding intensely to your son's intense reactions, and so forth. It could also be that your child's traits and behaviors affect you and your husband differently. You both may want to review Chapter Two to reconsider how your son's temperament influences you and your responses to him.

Our difficult child occupies so much of our attention we fear we are neglecting our other children. What can we do about this?

This problem may be unavoidable to some extent. Some children have high needs for attention and supervision that will consume a disproportionate amount of parents' time, just as though the child had a chronic physical condition such as diabetes or asthma. The best strategy would involve enlisting your spouse (and any professional advisors available to you) to help find ways of making your involvement with this challenging child as effective and efficient as possible so that it does not monopolize any more of your time than necessary. This is a major challenge for any parent.

At the same time, it is beneficial to plan ways of making certain that your involvement with the other children is as full and rewarding as possible for all concerned. A relatively smaller amount of "quality time" may be sufficient for an easier child.

Our difficult child usually starts the sibling battles. Although we try to deal with the children in an even-handed way, we end up making the innocent one feel guilty. How can we break this pattern?

First, consider whether the milder, more pleasant child is completely guiltless. That child may be angry about or jealous of the attention the more demanding child receives and may be quietly provoking their fights.

When it is necessary to intervene in a major sibling quarrel, do your best to administer justice evenly. It does not help to open with the question "Who started this?" Try to avoid the blame game and instead guide your children toward finding and negotiating their own solutions.

Your strategy with your easier child should probably include these additional steps:

- In a quiet, private moment, discuss with her the fact that her brother is quite different and has special needs. Especially if she is an older child, it is appropriate to acknowledge to her that you often find it hard to deal with him, but without using unflattering labels. Perhaps suggest some coping strategies you are using yourself.

- Emphasize that you are just as interested in meeting her needs and explain how you are trying to go about it. You do not want your easier child to develop the self-image of an abused saint or martyr.

- Special time alone with your easier child will be pleasant for both of you and can demonstrate your affection for her.

How can I not feel angry, frustrated, and inadequate with a child who is challenging?

Be honest with yourself about the way your child makes you feel. Try to liberate yourself from the uncomfortable feelings that may arise from mistaken notions such as these: fear that there is something wrong with your child, guilt that you are responsible for your child's temperament, or anger that your child is deliberately acting this way just to torment you.

Even when you step back and objectively evaluate your child's temperament and recognize that these traits are part and parcel of who he is, you still are often left with the annoyance and fatigue that comes with taking care of him. These feelings can diminish and your sense of self-confidence can increase as you understand more fully how your child's temperament functions and how best to handle it. Remember, too, that the difficult traits in a baby or toddler tend to lessen with time. Group discussions with other parents facing the same kinds of problems can be enormously helpful.

My doctor says I am depressed because of my baby. What am I to do?

If you think your doctor is correct, two steps are called for:

- Get help from someone who knows more about how to understand and manage a baby. This may be as simple as asking for the advice of more experienced parents who have been through this with their own children. Do not pay any mind to the professional or amateur who calls you a bad parent or places all the blame on you.

- If the depression is interfering with your life as a spouse and a parent, or with your job, seek professional help. As long as you remain significantly depressed you will also have increased difficulty understanding and dealing with your baby.

My child is very inflexible and negative. How can I calmly and wisely discipline him? I have been having such difficulty.

If this were easy, you would not be reaching out for answers now. Techniques for management have been explained in Chapters Three and Four. Remember that even the most experienced, self-confident parents have bad days with generally "easy" children. With those youngsters who present more challenges, you have to expect that there will be some rough spots no matter how informed and experienced you are as a parent. If your ability to discipline effectively is impaired by some uncomfortable feelings generated from your own childhood experiences, then perhaps you should seek counseling.

My baby is very hard for me to handle, but my mother keeps telling me that she thinks he is the best baby in the world. I do not know whether to believe her.

Remember that your mother (or mother-in-law, aunt, neighbor, or anyone else offering unsolicited commentary) may have forgotten what babies are like. She may think that any grandchild of hers has to be perfect, or she may be just trying to cheer you up. Whatever her reasons, do not let her confuse you. Instead, observe your baby and profile her temperament as outlined in Chapter One. This should help you accurately size up your baby's traits. Also ask a few experienced friends what they think; they should be able to give you an honest estimate unclouded by emotional issues.

My father-in-law says that I should just smack my son when he misbehaves. Is that really the right thing to do?

Resorting to physical violence is a bad way to raise a healthy child. At best, it makes a child stop briefly from some undesirable behavior. It does not work in the long run, and it does not teach anything positive. It only sends the message that hitting is acceptable behavior. Nevertheless, many parents use spanking and report that it does no harm. In any case, physical violence certainly does not improve a child's challenging temperament. Review Chapter Three for more effective ways of management and discipline.

My sister-in-law thinks that her sweet, adaptable infant is hard to manage. What can I do to help her see how lucky she is?

Tell her of your different view and why you think you are right. Get other credible people to do the same. Give her the chance to observe and profile her baby's temperament, as suggested in Chapter One. Also bear in mind that while she may not know much about babies, particularly if this is her first, the real problem may be that she has some personal problem that is interfering with her ability to appreciate this pleasant infant. It could be postpartum depression, marital problems, financial difficulties, or other factors that are upsetting her. If that appears to be the case, she should consider seeking counseling.

I sometimes feel as though I am letting my fussy baby run my life, and this cannot be good for me, or anyone. How can I keep from spoiling her with too much attention?

A challenging infant or toddler can take up a great deal of parents' time and attention. Your guideline should be that you try to meet your child's needs responsibly and sensitively. Attempt to read your child's real requirements, and do not let yourself be carried away by all the noise. Spoiling means different things to different people. The clearest definition is probably the situation that develops when parents yield to her whims. The child gets the impression that all she has to do is yell or fuss and the world will quickly comply with her demands. To avoid such situations, attend to her real needs without giving in every time she wants to be picked up, played with, entertained, or fed.

Our child often has intense, negative reactions and behaviors. This makes my wife and me extremely angry—to the point, I'm afraid, of shouting back at him and sometimes even spanking him. We know we should not let him reduce us to his childish level or to physical punishment, but what can we do in the heat of the moment?

When a child's typical response to parents' discipline and care giving efforts is intense and negative, it severely taxes parents' ability to provide affection and calm, nurturing guidance. Let's not underestimate the way this challenges and drains parents' methods of handling such a child.

Many parents find themselves being drawn into angry shouting matches and physical punishments that, in calmer moments, they know are not appropriate for responsible parenting. Some parents who are under very great emotional strain may go so far as to abuse a child physically or psychologically in these situations. While we can sympathize with their anger and frustration, we cannot excuse this lack of restraint that leads to the abuse.

Most parents are able to stop short of abuse, but some still find themselves yelling back at a child who has just yelled at them. When you recognize that this is happening, you should separate briefly. If your child is an infant or toddler, put him in the safety of a crib or playpen, go to another room, and shut the door. Take several minutes for yourself. When you are calmer, return to the child. If your child is older, tell him, "We are both so upset that we need to be apart for a little while. I am going to leave the room for ten minutes. We'll discuss how to solve this problem when I come back."

After the storm has blown over, a wise course would be to discuss the problem of how to handle your angry responses with someone, your spouse or an experienced friend who can help provide some perspective. You not only want to break your pattern of overreacting, you also want to learn how to read the underlying message that prompted your child's shouting. For the next time, you want to be ready to respond calmly to that message and not to the static created by his loud outbursts.

For example, if your child has just screamed a refusal to put on the clothes that you want him to wear, you may want to offer another outfit instead of screaming back out of sheer annoyance. By giving this some advance consideration, you will be better able to sort out which issues are important enough to take a stand on and which are not.

If there is any risk that you might harm your child, seek professional help right away.

If my baby's colic was due in part to her temperament and the temperament stays with her, why is the colic gone now?

For some reason—probably the maturation of the nervous system—the temperamental predisposition and the input of stimuli no longer are translated into excessive crying after three or four months of age. If you were successful at reading your baby's needs and were able to decrease the stimulation and increase the soothing sufficiently, the colicky crying should have diminished or stopped well before three or four months. Yet it is likely that the temperamental differences such as high sensitivity or greater irritability are still observable.

The day care teachers say my boy is aggressive. Is this his temperament or is it a behavioral problem?

First of all, find out what they mean by "aggressive." Ask them to describe specific examples, rather than just applying the term. If they mean simply that he is energetic, runs around a great deal, and sometimes accidentally runs into people or things, that is probably his temperament. If you have observed and profiled his temperament as outlined in Chapter One, you probably have found him to be rather active. This sort of aggressiveness is normal and should not be suppressed, only redirected so that he does not hurt himself or others in any way.

However, if the teachers cite examples of his being frequently offensive to other children or quarrelsome with them (like hitting, biting, or kicking), then he has a behavioral problem. It could mean either that he has not yet learned enough social skills or that he is upset by some stress in his life. This type of antisocial behavior should be taken seriously and steps taken to eliminate it. He needs to be guided toward more appropriate social behavior. You and the teachers should discuss ways of handling these behaviors in a consistent way at home and at the day care center.

My child is not one to adapt to things easily. She is so insistent that her friends do things her way that they do not want to play with her. Is this just a temperament problem or something worse?

Children who have trouble adapting to change, novelty, and the wishes of others are in danger of being unpopular if this tendency dominates their relations with other children. We expect all children (and all adults) to want to do things in their preferred ways; however, one of the tasks of growing up is learning to give in to what other people want, at least part of the time, in order to get along with them.

If a child insists so strongly on having her way that her friends are deserting her, she has a behavioral problem. She needs help in learning to become more flexible so that she will not become permanently estranged from her peers. It may not come easily to her, but she should be able to see that the sacrifice is better than social isolation. Try to work with her, in age-appropriate ways, to teach social skills of sharing and taking turns, to consider other children's wishes, and to accept that everyone must give and take in order to get along together.

If there is a behavioral adjustment problem, why does the child's temperament matter? Doesn't the therapist end up giving the same advice anyway?

It does matter because there is a difference between the management of the adjustment problem and the temperament risk factor. A knowledge of temperament helps in understanding why one child responds to a particular stress with a behavior disturbance, whereas another child is not bothered by it. The temperamental predisposition also accounts to some extent for the quality and intensity of the behavioral problem.

The therapist or counselor should be able to distinguish between the reactive behavioral problem, which is changeable, and the temperament, which is not. For example, the professional advisor can help a family handle a child's negative reaction to the arrival of a new sibling, but the advisor should also understand that the low adaptability (if that is part of the problem) will continue after the sibling rivalry has abated.

If a child refuses to go to school, is that just temperament or is it something else?

At the beginning of the school year, a child who is reluctant to go to school, or who cries or does not want to be left alone at school, may just be timid. Part of this child's temperament involves a slowness to accept new situations. Such a child, if well handled, will eventually accept the new place and gradually work his way into the group and the school routine. Usually, such a child previously has shown similar tendencies of being "slow to warm up."

A child who refuses outright to go to school at the beginning of or at other times during the school year—without having displayed this tendency in the past—may have a more serious condition called school avoidance or school refusal. This child may or may not have a shy temperament, but his main problem usually turns out to be anxiety about something that is going on at home, in school, on the way to school, or on the way home. A professional evaluation is generally advisable.

Isn't the most important issue the fit between the parent's temperament and the child's temperament?

Extensive studies of the match between the parent's and child's temperaments have not been conducted. However, clinical evidence to date suggests that the friction with a child's temperament is not primarily a result of the conflict with the parent's temperament but, rather, with the parent's values and expectations.

If a parent values and wants a mild temperament, and the child turns out to be intense, we do not know how much it matters whether the parent herself is mild or intense. We do know that the parent did not get what she preferred and may therefore have a problem in the relationship if she does not accept her child's given temperament and work with it. Problems may occur when the child has a great deal of an undesired trait or the parent has a special intolerance for it, or both.

Whose fault is it when there is tension between a spirited child and the parents?

Let's not dwell on fault or blame. Stress and conflict are inevitable even in the best relationships between parent and child. As a child grows older, parents' previous expectations continue and new ones arise for ever higher levels of performance in school and maturity in behavior. Dealing with a child who has a spirited temperament (one with such traits as high intensity, persistence, activity, and low adaptability) can be challenging for parents, and this can complicate the relationship.

Whether the stress and conflict are normal or excessive will depend on the harmony or disharmony that the parents promote by their ability to modify their interactions with their child to improve the fit. A young child cannot help her temperament. Adults, however, have a greater responsibility and capacity to alter their own behavior—disciplinary strategies—to bring greater harmony to the relationship with their child.

Is it true that the first two or three years of life are the most important for a child's adjustment?

The first years are very important to a child's physical, social, cognitive, and emotional development. A great deal of important growth and development also takes place after the infant and toddler periods. It is important to remember that even if you have made some mistakes in the early care of your child, there is a good chance that improved management can make things better both for your child and for your relationship with him.

I was disturbed to learn from a friend that children with "difficult" temperaments are more likely to become criminals with they grow up. Is this true?

No evidence exists to support this unfortunate rumor. Children with challenging temperament traits, such as slow adaptation and frequent negative moods, are more likely to develop social behavioral problems, such as aggressiveness, during early and middle childhood. These disturbances are generally much reduced or completely gone by adolescence, although a minority of children continue to have adjustment problems.

The overwhelming weight of evidence is that unfavorable environmental factors are the primary reason children turn to delinquency or criminal behavior.

Our daughter's behavioral problem is better now, thanks to a successful intervention by a psychologist. But she is still difficult to manage. How long should we continue with therapy?

If the behavioral problem has been largely solved by changes in your management of her, and you have a good idea of how it got started and how to avoid a repetition, then you probably have completed the intervention. You are not going to change her temperament by parent counseling or psychotherapy; you will have to live with it.

Therefore, be sure you have enough information about how to deal with her particular temperament and any other issues, then discuss discontinuing the sessions with the psychologist with well-deserved thanks.

"Time-out" does not work with our child. Why are we having such trouble using this technique when it seems to work well for other families?

Most often, when parents say that time-out does not work, it is because they are not using it correctly. You should review the technique with someone who really knows how to use it to find out what you may be doing wrong. Are you applying the technique consistently? Are you using it for every little infraction, so frequently that is has lost its effectiveness? Do you sometimes back down when your child begs to be let out of time-out? Are you making it clear that time-out is given as a consequence for a specific, unacceptable behavior?

If you are doing everything right and still having trouble making this technique work, it may be that your child is highly intense and persistent, rather negative and not very adaptable. If these barriers are obstructing progress, you will have to be more firm and rigorous in applying the rules for time-out. You may also need to seek some professional help.

My child is somewhat difficult, and his behavior worries me. Every time I decide to get professional help, though, he seems to get better. What is going on here?

How challenging his temperament seems may vary, depending on how resourceful and supported you are feeling at the time. Another possibility is that his shifting situation, together with his unchanging temperament, is producing intermittent adjustment problems such as sleep disturbances or bouts of aggressiveness. In the latter case, when you put your mind to the problem to figure out what is going on and what you can do about it, you could be adjusting his care just enough to make the problem go away—until a new challenge comes along to take its place. This is a common pattern.

Do difficult children develop a poor self-image? Are there certain temperament traits that affect a child's self-esteem?

We need some studies to answer this important question with the detail it deserves. It seems to make sense that if a child is frequently generating friction with the people around her and is getting harsh words from them in return, then she may tend to feel that the world does not like her very much.

A child who invites negative, critical responses from parents and other significant adults probably forms a more negative image of herself than does a child whose pleasant manner attracts smiles and affection. Whenever a child exhibits temperament traits that annoy you, it is therefore important to recognize that these traits should not be labeled with derogatory words such as "lazy," "wild," "stubborn," and so on. You need to work toward improving the fit between those inborn traits and your parenting approach without damaging your child's self-esteem. Criticism should be directed at the unacceptable behavior, not at your child. Practice responding in neutral terms to her when she behaves in ways that bother you. You can help enhance her self-esteem by praising her truly positive traits and behaviors.

What is wrong with labeling a child "difficult" if he or she really is difficult?

There is a difference between a label and a description. In this case, the label is a general term used to define a group of children with certain characteristics that most parents find hard to manage. The danger is that the label may be too simplistic or not sufficiently individualized, or it may be misleading. And although the expression of the temperament may change, the label can still stick.

One person's notion of what makes a child hard to manage may not be the same as that of another. There is also a real danger that such a term may be misused in an uncomplimentary way. It may encourage parents to respond in ways that are not justified by the child's actual behavior. My preference is to use descriptive terms that more precisely reflect the trait or style of behavior (for example, "relatively slow to adjust to change" or "somewhat more active than average") and to avoid labels such as "difficult" as much as possible. In this way, there is much less chance misunderstanding the term and of stereotyping the child.

I know my child's temperament is not the easiest, but the teacher is not knowledgeable about temperament and says she is disturbed by his behavior. What can I do?

It is a distressing situation when you feel that you know more about your child's temperament and behavior than the teacher does. Your best bet is to tell the teacher what you know about your child's temperament and to explain the successful methods you have developed to deal with challenging behaviors. This may help the teacher become more aware of the normality of your child.

If that does not help, discuss the matter with the guidance counselor, school psychologist, or principal. If you are correct, these possibly more experienced personnel may be able to enlighten the inexperienced teacher. If they all agree that your child is, in fact, having significant adjustment problems, then you need to revise your estimate and consider seeking an outside professional evaluation and, if necessary, help for your child.

Last year's teacher said my son was able to concentrate well. But his new teacher this year says he is too inattentive. How can that be?

Several explanations are possible. This may simply be a difference of opinion between two teachers, which is a common occurrence. Or, the new teacher may have different classroom rules that require your son to adjust. It is also possible your child has changed. Perhaps he has become worried, tired, or sick, and thus may actually be less attentive in school than he was last year. Also consider that the new classroom situation could hold more distractions for him, such as noises, more disruptive children—or members of the opposite sex. Still another possibility is that the level of academic work has increased to a point where his learning abilities are being taxed more heavily.

Because there are a variety of possible explanations, you should not assume that there is a single, simple answer that fits everyone. Stay in touch with your son's new teacher to see how she is handling the classroom situation, and learn how you can work together to help your son increase his attention to schoolwork.

School personnel say I should be happy about the diagnosis of ADHD because that means my son's problem is neither my fault nor theirs, but is all in his brain chemistry. Are they right?

Up to a point. It is a relief for parents and teachers to understand that a child's poor school performance is not all their fault. However, this view overlooks the fact that the difference in the child's functioning, whether from an actual abnormality in the brain or more likely from a normal variation in temperament, does not express itself in a vacuum. In other words, it interacts with the environment. Parents, therefore, are responsible for helping inattentive or inflexible children find ways of meeting school requirements. And teachers and school administrators are responsible for making the school environment flexible enough to accommodate the broad range of normal behavioral and learning styles. Unfortunately, such help often is available only when a diagnosis such as ADHD has been made.

We are having a great many problems in managing our child at home, but the teacher says she is doing just fine. How can that be?

The first question is whether she really is behaving differently. That is best determined by discussing her behavior with the teacher. If she does appear to change when in the two places, it could be that the dissimilar setting and handling at school bring out a side of her that you have not seen much of at home. A bright child may do better at school because she is happier there with the intellectual challenge.

She also may be putting on her best manners at school. Or she may be performing exactly the same at school, and the teacher views it differently. For example, her boldness and intensity may be valued at school, whereas you may prefer her to behave in a more subdued style.

Our daughter does not seem very bothered by the new baby. We cannot figure out whether she is really taking it well or just concealing her anger about being displaced as the center of attention in the family.

Be thankful that things are going well. The adaptability of an older child makes the process of family growth much easier. If your daughter does not appear bothered, that is probably the way it is. Little children tend not to be very good actors and, if there is any anger, it usually shows through rather clearly in one way or another. It sounds as though your child is adapting well to the new baby. Remember, however, that sibling relations evolve and change over time. If you have not already profiled her temperament traits, you may want to observe her responses in a variety of different situations to determine her overall adaptability trait.

CONCLUSION: WHAT WE CAN DO WITH WHAT WE KNOW

Although our knowledge of temperament is incomplete, in these pages we have tried to present the best information available to help you recognize and evaluate temperament differences in your children. Even if you have not become an expert at this process, you are the world's greatest authority about your own child. You are in a position to couple your insight into your child with the information presented here to improve your understanding of temperament differences and their potential consequences.

You are now likely to be far more able to manage your child's behavior. The new ideas about management you have gathered can make raising your child less troublesome for you. And you are now more skillful at solving your child's adjustment problems when they involve temperament–environment clashes and when they are not too severe. Hopefully, you now recognize more clearly the difference between what you can do yourself and what may require the help of a mental health professional.

If the teachers, child care workers, relatives, doctors, nurses, coaches, and others you deal with are well informed about temperament and the importance of a good fit, both you and your child are indeed fortunate. Many of these people who interact with your child are not informed. By sharing your knowledge and the ways in which it is helping you and your child, you can tactfully assist professionals in broadening their knowledge, just as you have broadened yours.

Temperament is a highly complex matter. By acknowledging its central importance and understanding its nature, you are able to handle your child's behavior with far greater precision. And you are less likely to blame irrelevant influences, such as the circumstances of your baby's delivery or your child's diet. Knowledge of temperament also helps you sort out which aspects of your child's behavior need immediate attention and which ones can be attended to later. This prioritizing can lead to a reduction in stress around the home.

Many have said it, and it remains true: Parenting is one of the most difficult and rewarding jobs for any human being. Fulfilling children's physical, emotional, social, and developmental needs and steering them toward acceptable patterns of behavior—especially in today's fragmented society—is an enormous challenge. Having a clearer understanding of what makes your children respond the way they do and also having more effective strategies and tactics for handling behavior concerns will help you meet this challenge. Instead of relying on a rigid formula for responding to various behaviors, you are now able to manage some of your child's areas of conflict by adjusting the specific situation. If the issue is one of fit, the solution lies in recognizing and accommodating it.

If this book achieves anything, it will be to convince parents that they can become better caregivers and happier adults who are in charge of their lives. Their children will benefit immensely from their parents' greater competence and contentment.

The ultimate message of this book is this: *Work with your child's temperament, not against it.* Temperament is the continuing core of a child's personality that shapes experiences throughout life. If we understand, tolerate, and respect children's individual temperaments, we will give them a lifelong gift of acceptance.

We began this book with the visual image of a quilt composed of nine patches. We would like to leave you with another image, one borrowed from Ralph Waldo Emerson, the eminent American writer. In his 1844 essay "Experience," Emerson spoke of life's experiences as "a train of moods like a string of beads." What ties these experiences together, he wrote, "depends on the structure or temperament. Temperament is the iron wire on which the beads are strung."

As you work with your child's temperament, perhaps you will think of the shape and durability of the "iron wire" and appreciate how it organizes and gives a pattern to the "beads" of experience.

RESOURCES

OTHER BOOKS FOR PARENTS ABOUT TEMPERAMENT AND ITS MANAGEMENT

Brazelton, T. Berry. *Infants and Mothers: Differences in Development.* New York: Delacorte, 1969.

Budd, Linda S. *Living with the Active Alert Child: Groundbreaking Strategies for Parents,* revised and enlarged edition. Seattle, WA: Parenting Press, 1993.

Chess, Stella, and Alexander Thomas. *Know Your Child.* New York: Basic Books, 1987. Republished, New Brunswick, NJ: Jason Aronson, 1996.

Chess, Stella, Alexander Thomas, and Herbert G. Birch. *Your Child Is a Person.* New York: Viking, 1965.

Forehand, Rex, and Nicholas Long. *Parenting the Strong-Willed Child.* Chicago, IL: Contemporary Books, 1996.

Greenspan, Stanley I., and Jacqueline Salmon. *The Challenging Child: Understanding, Raising, and Enjoying the Five "Difficult" Types of Children.* Reading, MA: Addison-Wesley, 1995.

Kurcinka, Mary Sheedy. *Raising Your Spirited Child.* New York: HarperCollins, 1991.

Sears, William. *The Fussy Baby: How to Bring Out the Best in Your High-Need Child.* New York: New American Library/Signet, 1989.

Turecki, Stanley, with Leslie Tonner. *The Difficult Child,* revised edition. New York: Bantam Books, 1989.

Zimbardo, Philip G., and Shirley L. Radl. *The Shy Child: A Parent's Guide to Overcoming and Preventing Shyness from Infancy to Adulthood.* New York: Dolphin, 1981.

VIDEOTAPES

California Department of Education. *Flexible, Fearful, or Feisty: The Temperaments of Infants and Toddlers.* Sacramento, CA: California Department of Education, 1989. California Department of Education, P.O. Box 944272, Sacramento, CA 94244-2720. Useful for parents and child care workers.

Audio-Visual Department, Oakland, CA: Kaiser Permanente Health Plan, 1995. Audio-Visual Department, Kaiser Permanente Health Plan, 1950 Franklin Street, Oakland, CA 94612. A series of four tapes primarily for health care providers; parents may also find them useful.

PARENT SELF-HELP GROUPS AND INFORMATION ABOUT HOW TO START THEM

Center for Human Development, Temperament Program, 1100 K Avenue, La Grande, Oregon 97850.

Kurcinka, Mary Sheedy. *Raising Your Child: The Next Step. (working title)* New York: HarperCollins. A workbook for parents to be published in 1998.

The Temperament Project, C/O Variety Child Development Centre, 9460 140th Street, Surrey, British Columbia, V3V 5Z4, Canada.

BOOKS ABOUT HANDLING BEHAVIORAL PROBLEMS IN CHILDREN

Many useful books have been published about children's behavior. In only one of these, however, has a significant effort been made to include temperament as part of the assessment and management of behavior:

Turecki, Stanley, and Sarah Wernick. *Normal Children Have Problems, Too: How Parents Can Understand and Help.* New York: Bantam, 1994.

This book provides guidelines for parents in attempting to solve their children's less severe behavior problems. Despite the good sense of the technique proposed in the book, it must be acknowledged that the success rate of the plan has not been formally evaluated.

Most of the other books about behavior problems mention little or nothing at all about temperament. Yet they do offer good general advice about behavior management. A sampling of the better ones is included below.

Baker, Bruce L., et al. *Behavior Problems.* Champaign, IL: Research Press, 1976.

Blechman, Elaine A. *Solving Child Behavior Problems at Home and at School.* Champaign, IL: Research Press, 1985.

Christophersen, Edward R. *Little People: Guidelines for Commonsense Child Rearing,* 3rd edition. Kansas City, KA: Westport, 1988.

Garber, Stephen W., et al. *Good Behavior.* New York: Villard Books, 1987.

Green, Christopher. *Toddler Taming: A Guide to Your Child from One to Four.* New York: Ballantine, 1990.

Philadelphia Child Guidance Center. *Your Child's Emotional Health.* New York: Macmillan, 1993.

Samalin, Nancy, with Martha M. Jablow. *Loving Your Child Is Not Enough: Positive Discipline That Works.* New York: Viking Penguin, 1987. Penguin Books, 1988.

FURTHER RESEARCH DATA

For readers who want to learn more of the technical background of this book, the most useful single summary of the research data on which this book is based is the first book listed below, in which readers will find twenty-three pages of references. The second book listed below is the other most comprehensive summary of current research.

Carey, William B., and Sean C. McDevitt. *Coping with Children's Temperament: A Guide for Professionals.* New York: Basic Books, 1995.

Kohnstamm, Geldolph A., John E. Bates, and Mary K. Rothbart, editors. *Temperament in Childhood.* New York: John Wiley & Sons, 1989.

PROFESSIONAL MEASUREMENTS OF YOUR CHILD'S TEMPERAMENT

In talking with a pediatrician, psychologist, or educator, it may be suggested to you that your child's temperament be formally assessed. To obtain the best measurement, your professional advisor would be wise to use one of the standardized questionnaires presently available to clinicians and teachers for use in their offices and classrooms. The parent questionnaires cover the same behaviors that you rated in Chapter One; however, the scoring of a set of standardized items allows comparisons with a large number of other children. The teacher questionnaires concentrate on traits observed in school that are important for work there.

QUESTIONNAIRES COMPLETED BY PARENTS

These five different scales cover ages one month to 12 years and are completely consistent with the descriptions of temperament characteristics used in this book. They can be obtained from two separate sources:

> Behavioral/Developmental Initiatives East
> Suite 131, 1316 West Chester Pike
> West Chester, PA 19382
> Telephone: 800-BDI-8303; fax: 610-296-1325
> e-mail: 74261.444@compuserve.com

> Behavioral/Developmental Initiatives of Arizona
> Suite 104, 13802 North Scottsdale Road
> Scottsdale, AZ 85254
> Telephone: 800-405-2313; fax: 602-494-2688
> e-mail: bdi@primenet.com

BDI, for which the senior author is an advisor but neither an owner nor an investor, also offers a computer scoring system either for use in the professional's office or for faxing to BDI for rapid processing and turnaround. If your clinician does not offer this service, see about a referral to another professional who does. BDI discourages parents from applying directly.

QUESTIONNAIRES FOR TEACHERS

Educators can obtain a different set of scales appropriate for ratings and scoring by teachers and counselors in school. The Temperament Assessment Battery for Children by Professor Roy Martin and associates is available from

> Pro-Ed Publishers
> 8700 Shoal Creek Boulevard
> Austin, TX 78757
> Telephone: 512-451-3246

PROFESSIONAL ADVISORS

It would be highly desirable if one could list several competent advisors on temperament issues, at least in the major population areas of the country. Unfortunately, no such list exists at this time. Your child's physician should know of any trained advisors in your area. In the meantime, you may wish to consult the BDI website on the Internet maintained by my colleague, Dr. Sean C. McDevitt, which provides a brief list of such advisors:

> BDI website address: http://www.b-di.com

INDEX

Abdominal pain, 126–27
Academic performance, *see* School
  performance
Accidents and injuries, 41, 122–23
Activity, 5–7, 24–25, 53,
  61–64, 85
Adaptability, 10–12, 27–28, 54,
  69–72, 86, 177–78, 206, 216
Adjustment, behavioral, *see*
  Behavior
Adolescents, 5, 13–14, 21–23, 82,
  150
Adoption, 169
Affection, xx, 37, 42, 44–45, 58
Aggression, 47, 92, 166, 195, 205
Anxiety, 133, 155, 158, 163, 208
Approach, *see* Initial reaction,
Attention Deficit/Hyperactivity
  Disorder (ADHD), xiv, xxii,
  151–59, 177, 189, 215
Attention span, *see* Persistence

Barkley, Russell, 156
Bedwetting, *see* Enuresis
Behavior, 89–105
  adjustment, xix, 47, 92–105, 207
  components, 92–93
  differences from temperament,
    92, 178
  effects of temperament on, xxii,
    94–97
  management of problems in,
    97–105
  in school, 150–51
  social behavior, 92–93, 206–7

Birth order, 186
Body (circadian) rhythms, 125
Brazelton, T. Berry, xvi

Caries (cavities), bottle–mouth,
  see Dental decay
Chess, Stella, iii, xiv, xv, xxii, 4, 18,
  94–95, 104, 114, 148
Child care, *see* Daycare
Clusters of traits, xxvi, 18, 81, 114
Colic, xi, 123–25, 136, 205
Coping style, 93
Crises, 161–72

da Vinci, Leonardo, 52–53
Daycare, 139–44, 192
Dental decay, 39, 130
Depression, 94, 155, 158,
  163, 201
Development, effects of
  temperament on, 42,
  107–17
Diagnostic and Statistical Manuals,
  153–54
"Difficult" temperament, xxvii,
  18, 51, 54, 95, 114, 122,
  129, 185–86, 197,
  210–13
Disabilities, developmental, 107,
  112–17
Disasters, 162, 165, 169–70
Discipline, xx, 43–44, 57, 69, 103,
  201–2, 204
Distractibility, 15–16, 31–32, 51,
  56, 77–79, 87

ABOUT THE AUTHORS

William B. Carey, M.D., is Director of Behavioral Pediatrics in the Division of General Pediatrics at The Children's Hospital of Philadelphia and Clinical Professor of Pediatrics at the University of Pennsylvania School of Medicine, Philadelphia, Pennsylvania.

Dr. Carey received the C. Anderson Aldrich Award from the American Academy of Pediatrics in 1991 for "outstanding contributions in the field of child development," the AAP's highest accolade in the child development area. Other recipients have included Dr. Benjamin Spock, Anna Freud, Erik Erikson, and Dr. T. Berry Brazelton.

The AAP also recognized Dr. Carey in 1992 with its Practitioner Research Award for the behavioral research he has conducted for three decades. Working in a solo pediatric practice and collaborating with psychologists, he developed a set of questionnaires for professionals to use in identifying and evaluating the variety of children's temperaments. These diagnostic tools, which have been translated into some thirty languages, are used worldwide by physicians and mental health professionals. In 1984, he was elected to the Institute of Medicine of the National Academy of Sciences.

A pediatrician since 1955, Dr. Carey has written and edited five professional books and more than ninety-five papers and chapters on the subject of children's temperament and other behavioral and developmental issues. His most recent book, *Coping with Children's Temperaments: A Guide for Professionals*, was written with psychologist Sean C. McDevitt and published in 1995.

Dr. Carey is a graduate of Yale University and the Harvard Medical School and had his pediatric training at The Children's Hospital of Philadelphia. He and his wife, Ann, live in Swarthmore, Pennsylvania, and have three adult daughters and one grandchild.

Dr. Carey's collaborator, Martha M. Jablow, has written five nonfiction books: *Teenage Healthcare*, with Dr. Gail B. Slap; *A Parent's Guide to Eating Disorders and Obesity* for The Children's Hospital of Philadelphia series; *One in a Million*, with Harry A. Cole; *Loving Your Child Is Not Enough*, with Nancy Samalin; *Cara: Growing With a Retarded Child*; and the Introduction to the 1992 reissue of *The Child Who Never Grew* by Pearl S. Buck.

She and her husband, Paul, have two adult children and live in Philadelphia.